MA T

CHECK CD AT END

TRANSITIONS

A COMPREHENSIVE INDEPENDENCE PLAY-ALONG SYSTEM

by RUSS MILLER

- The prequel to the critically acclaimed *The Drum Set Crash Course.*

- A complete independence system from two limbs to four limbs.

- Play-along tracks for every exercise!

- Teaches you to play music while building independence and facility.

Editors: Russ Miller/Ray Brych
Project Manager: Ray Brych
Production Coordinator: Edmond Randle
Art Design & Layout: María A. Chenique
Engraver: Adrián Álvarez

NOTATION CHART

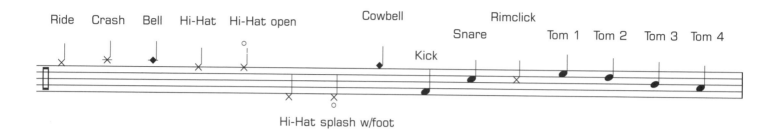

Ride   Crash   Bell   Hi-Hat   Hi-Hat open   Cowbell   Rimclick   Snare   Tom 1   Tom 2   Tom 3   Tom 4

Kick

Hi-Hat splash w/foot

DRUM SET NOTATION EXAMPLE

By using the notation chart, here is an example of a common drum set notation.
Not only is the placement of notes in the beats important, but so is the voicing of the notes
on the drum set.

CREDITS AND INFORMATION:

CD Recorded at R.M.I. Music Productions Chatsworth, CA
Mastered at R.M.I. Music Productions
Engineered and produced by Russ Miller

All drum set examples and song tracks by Russ Miller

Eighth-note play-alongs:	Guitar—Gannin Arnold Bass—Don Patterson
Eighth-note play-along song:	Guitars—Gannin Arnold Bass—Jonathan Ahrens
Eighth-note triplet play-alongs:	Guitar—Gannin Arnold Bass—Don Patterson Saxes—George Shelby
Eighth-note triplet play-along song:	"Bimini" written by Rique Pantoja © 1991 Rique Pantoja music ASCAP Piano/Keyboards—Rique Pantoja Bass—Guillermo Guzman Sax—George Shelby
Sixteenth-note play-alongs:	Guitar—Gannin Arnold Bass—Don Patterson Saxes—George Shelby Trumpet—Lee Thornburg
Sixteenth-note play-along song:	"Brincaderia" written by Rique Pantoja © 1995 Rique Pantoja music ASCAP Piano/Keyboards—Rique Pantoja Bass—Guillermo Guzman Sax—George Shelby

Russ would like to personally thank: Jesus Christ for the gift of life and music. My beautiful wife Christine, you are the reason for everything I do. Fred Anton, Dave Hakim, Ray Brych, Mike Finkelstein, Gayle Geise, and all at Warner Bros. Publications. Hagi, Jerry Andreas, Joe Testa, and all at Yamaha Drums. Bob Yerby and Gavin Carignan and all at Remo drum heads. John Dechristopher, Colin Scofield, Jair Neciosup, and all at Zildjian cymbals. Randy and Lauren May at May mikes. Ryan Smith at Shure microphones. Terry Therion at Impact cases. Bob and Joann Gatzen at Drumframe, Joe Hernandez, Ramon Casales and all at MEINL Percussion. All at IMP Europe. Yamaha Japan, England, Italy, and France. Zoro, Jarod, and Renee Russo. Joe and Kim Testa. The Burwell and Niles families. My good friends, Rique Pantoja, Guillermo Guzman, George Shelby, Don Patterson, Gannin Arnold, Johnathan Ahrens, Lee Thornburg, Jeff Danna, and all of the great friends I play music with on a daily basis, thanks for your inspiration. I also would like to especially thank all of the students, fans, friends, and colleagues who have supported all of my products through the years. Thank you.

CONTENTS

FOREWORD

In my first book *The Drum Set Crash Course,* I focused on various attributes needed for a drummer to play several different music styles convincingly. When I thought further about the space restrictions of one book, I couldn't effectively communicate the important role that independence plays in mastering many styles. The system I devised for the funk chapter in the *Crash Course* book (titled "The Ghosting System") was an independence learning method that may be used for several styles. I was approached by several percussion teachers about how to help a student make the transition from a drum pad or snare drum (two-limb independence), to full drum kit facility (four-limb independence) required for much of today's drum set playing. Thus, *Transitions* was born!

The most important thing I always try to stress while doing clinics and teaching is the experiences of playing music. It was the fundamental undertone of the *Crash Course* book and of my second book, *The Commandments of R&B Drumming,* with my friend Zoro. I wanted to make a total play-along system for working on all of these boring independence exercises! Developing this facility on the drum set is very time-consuming and can be quite frustrating. This system was developed so that you will gain physical ability on the instrument while learning to listen and react within a musical context. The idea of these play-alongs are to hear where and how the abilities gained by these exercises will be used from a practical standpoint. When I was in a practice-intensive time in my career, I was always wondering, "When am I going to use this stuff?" I didn't find out until years later, when someone asked me to play certain figures, where the benefits of all the hard work would be effective. The systems in this book, along with the recorded tracks, are assembled from a musical perspective. All of the combinations will be used in a practical musical genre.

I highly recommend going through this text with the guidance of a private instructor. He or she will be able to help you focus on certain characters of each system that are impossible to put down on paper. This is where the recorded examples of exercises come into play. These tracks were recorded to give you sonic examples of these systems and play-alongs. This is for you to hear musical colors that can and should be a part of these exercises. Due to time restrictions on the CD, we could put only one tempo of each play-along on the accompanying disc. These tempos were chosen with a few factors in mind:

1. **The general tempo range of the specific play-along style**. Obviously, every style of music has many tempos, but for a general rule, most styles stay within certain B.P.M. ranges.
2. **Independence exercises are usually conquered in a few phases**. In the beginning of working on the exercise, you are usually just trying to get your limbs to move opposite of each other. There is no point in having a play-along's tempo be so slow that it would not be able to be used at this level. The second phase of conquering a system is the tempo range I chose for the play-

along. I feel that at these "medium" tempos are the point at which the artic-ulations and character are developed. This is where playing music with the patterns are the most important. I always say in my clinics, "Learning to play something fast is not difficult, but learning to play something well is very difficult." Many people think that playing a figure fast is the key to conquering them. This is very untrue; you can play anything quicker if you have the *correct* movements under your belt. These correct movements are easily done at quicker tempos. But if you try to speed up incorrect move-ments, they will get increasing harder. This is why I didn't put extremely up-tempo versions of each play-along on the disc.

3. **Play-alongs are meant to be used in several different ways**. You should go through the entire book as written. Use the play-alongs for lining up the various figures in the exercises. After you have gone through each section, you can then go back through the play-alongs using the tracks as set-up exercises. Play fills leading to each one of the figures. This method gets you used to feeling where these various figures land in the measures. The object of this is not to play through the tracks at quick tempos or with a noncha-lant attitude toward them but to really focus on how the figures fall in time. This internal sense of rhythmic figures helps you tremendously in sight-reading. When you are reading on the fly, you don't have time to analyze where figures fall. If you can be familiar with several different rhythmic combinations in the measures, you will have more of a natural feel of how to execute and play around all of these different rhythms.

I realize there is so much information that gets thrown at you in a method book. I recommend taking your time and not getting frustrated. Learning independence is an extremely physical task. You have to let your various limbs get used to making move-ments they have never made before. This takes some time to do. Everybody's bodies are different, so certain movements are easier for some than others. This book is meant to be a system that should take a long period of time to master. In an age when we are used to getting whatever we want extremely quickly, there are still things that are learned and accomplished with time and patience! This book is a prequel to *The Drum Set Crash Course* book I released previously. This book gives you the physical abilities to attack the conceptual attributes of the *Crash Course*. One of the keys to both of these books is to read through all of the text in each and really take time to think about what is being said in the exercise text and historical sections of the *Crash Course* book. Some things that are very important are not always easily written down. That's why I highly recommend checking out the *The Drum Set Crash Course* video. This tool gives you the visual and audio demonstrations that can help you master these exercises and music styles.

LINEAR EXERCISES

The term "linear" basically means **no** two limbs are playing notes simultaneously. The process of learning linear playing has two ability levels. We will be focusing on a form of basic linear playing I call "two-limb independence." Linear drumming has often been associated with complicated, funky, full drum kit patterns used mainly for the purpose of facility development. (Please refer to the linear study in the funk chapter of *The Drum Set Crash Course* book.) This form of drumming is challenging and usually approached at an intermediate to advanced level of study. I use the term "two-limb" to refer mainly to playing just a snare drum or drum pad. Theoretically, there is no independence unless one limb is playing a contra-rhythmic figure to the other limb. Let's look at this as a reference to two-limbs working together to play even flows of notes.

Transitions is a learning system focused on conquering the physical challenges of playing **music,** using independence studies as a foundation. One of the most crucial times in a drummer's studies is learning basic hand-to-hand figures. This ability will affect how you can play rhythms spread between multiple instruments of the drum kit. Many students overlook the importance of their drum pad studies, wanting to get to the full kit and groove! It is very important to work on these fundamental hand-to-hand movements so as not to hinder ourselves when our learning focus changes to all four limbs playing! I have been approached by several people at clinics and masterclasses asking about physical problems they are having. I know these "problems" stem from the most basic forms of drumming. It is very hard to go back and work on drum pad exercises when you have been playing a full kit for many years. The time to conquer these problems is in the beginning stages of learning. We must first and foremost have the ability and mental understanding to hear the basic flows of notes and create them with any sticking on a pad. Do not underestimate the difficulty of this. I'm not talking about barely executing eighth notes and then moving on. I'm talking about being able to create a solid flow of time and having the ability to accent any portion of the measure with any sticking. This understanding will open the door to using multiple limbs on any instrument of the drum kit and executing any figures required of us! This freedom from physical problems takes the focus off the drums and allows us to focus on playing the music! This "music first" approach is what *Transitions* and *The Drum Set Crash Course* system is all about. I have said repeatedly in my clinics that the most effective thing I ever learned in my career was the ability to play *music* first and drums second! This is why I chose to add *Transitions* to the *Crash Course* system. I want students to be able to focus on music at the very basic stages of playing drums. This will affect how you think of this instrument for the rest of your career.

When working on the following system, keep in mind a few main points:

1. Your right and left hands need to have as close to an equal amount of facility as possible.
2. You need to be able to play even flows of notes without recognizing there are changes in the stickings.
3. You need to be able to accent any partial of a measure using any sticking you can think of.
4. You need to have a solid time-keeping ability just between the two hands before you move to the full drum kit.
5. You need to develop a "feel" just with the two hands so you can later apply this to the full drum kit.

With all of these attributes of two-limb playing in mind, let's get started!

CHAPTER ONE
TWO-LIMB INDEPENDENCE
LINEAR EXERCISES, STRAIGHT EIGHTH NOTES

The first concept to focus on is the ability to play a very consistent straight eighth-note pulse. The term "straight eighth notes" refers to a flow of eighth notes spread exactly even across one measure of music. This flow of notes looks like this:

This very basic flow of notes should be practiced on a drum pad or snare drum along with a metronome set to play an eighth-note subdivision. Practice this from a B.P.M. (beats per minute) range of 60–180. It is very important for the notes being played to line up exactly with the clicks being made by the metronome. The first level of playing any flow of notes is to play it with just one hand. After working through many different B.P.M. settings with each hand separately, use an alternate sticking technique (R, L, R, L, etc.).

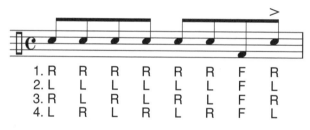

I highly recommend working closely with a private instructor through hand development books before attempting to learn full drum kit playing. This will help in challenges that are faced later in drum set studies. Ted Reed's *Syncopation* book is a great resource for learning different accent patterns in eighth-note flows. The next step after gaining the ability to play a very solid eighth-note pulse between the hands is to add in the kick drum foot.

This first eighth-note exercise is a basic interplay between the hands and one foot. The idea is very simple but is not simple to execute perfectly. The concept of playing extremely consistent flows of notes becomes increasingly more challenging as different limbs come into play. It is very easy to let the physical challenges stop the consistency in the note flow. (For instance, using the kick drum for some notes can easily cause a "weaving effect" in the time if not executed correctly.) The exercise is for the development of one accented note per bar. For the purpose of developing the note flows between the limbs, the kick will play the accented note.

DEVELOPMENTAL IDEA 💡

Singing the eighth-note flow aloud or just mentally while playing a consistent flow of notes will help you solidify the time. This mental focus will also help you lock in with the band.

EXERCISE TRACK (Track 2) & (Track 6)

1.R	R	R	R	R	R	R
2.L	L	L	L	L	L	L
3.R	L	R	L	R	L	R
4.L	R	L	R	L	R	L

This next exercise uses the same play-along track but has the kick playing the basic eighth-note flow. The snare will play the accented note. Play this exercise with the right hand playing the accented note; then replay it with the left hand playing the accented note.

EXERCISE TRACK (Track 2) & (Track 6)

The next step in the eighth-note development is using groups of two notes per measure. This brings up some unexpected challenges. It is very common to rush or play groups of two notes too quickly. This creates gaps in the flow of time. The notes are not being played exactly evenly throughout the measure. This is a very common mistake among players. Whenever groups of two notes are being played by the same limb, it becomes even more common to rush. Again, singing the flow of notes in your head or aloud is the best way to combat this habit. Remember to play through this exercise with the four recommended sticking patterns. Keep in mind that practicing these exercises at different tempos is very important. The play-along tempo is a medium B.P.M. Every possible tempo of play-along could not be put on a CD, so this medium tempo version is always just a center point to strive for and surpass.

DEVELOPMENTAL IDEA

One trick for not rushing groups of two notes with each hand is to slightly accent the second note. This gives the second note a concentrated value and doesn't make it a by-product of the first note.

EXERCISE TRACK

Here is the same concept of two-note groups played with the hands. Remember to use the four sticking patterns that are recommended for multiple-note hand figures (RR/LL/RL/LR). While playing these exercises with the CD play-along tracks, it is possible to hear the slight accent played by the bass guitar where each of the two-note group figures lie. All of the play-along tracks in *Transitions* have the band playing or "copying" the specific figures in each exercise. This unison playing becomes more important as the lessons progress.

EXERCISE TRACK (Track 8)

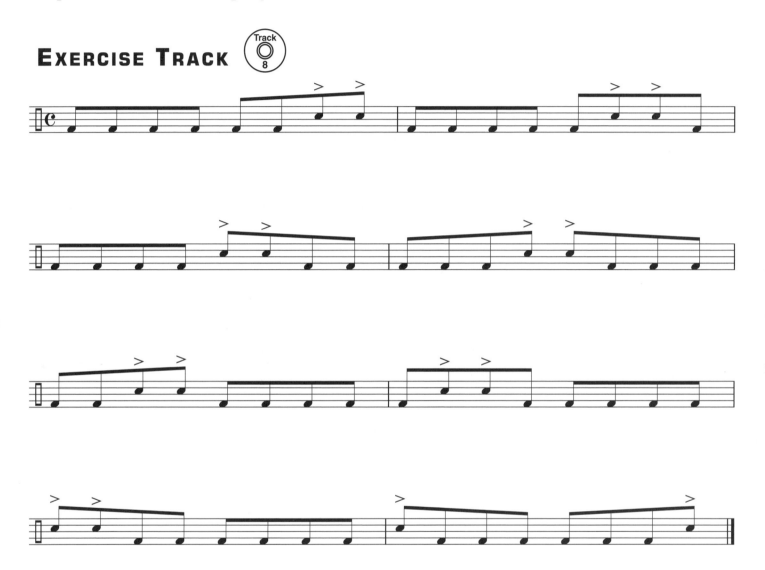

The next step is to add the third note into each measure. It becomes more and more difficult to keep the perfect spacing (or time-keeping) when more notes switch between limbs. Notice how the notes are not always grouped in three-note groups depending on their start position in the measure. There is still three notes in the measure being accented, but the group is broken up because of their measure position. Focus on basic counting/singing skills when the note figures become more difficult to read.

DEVELOPMENTAL IDEA 💡

When playing three-note groups with the same limb, try slightly accenting the third note in the group. Also, a slight crescendo (increasing from softer to louder) leading to the third note helps the figure sound more musical.

EXERCISE TRACK (Track 10)

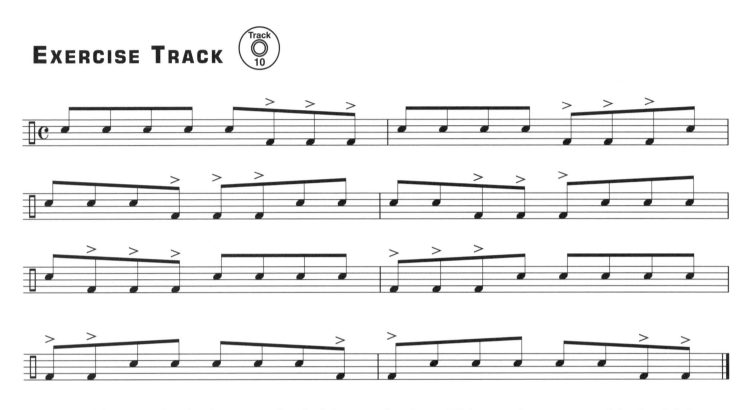

This exercise is the same basic idea as the last. This version starts with the kick drum. Remember to perform the slight crescendo and accent of the third note more than the others in the group.

EXERCISE TRACK (Track 10)

14

The four-note version of these exercises is the most challenging. The measure is split in half between kick drum notes and hand notes. At quicker tempos, the kick drum will be very challenging. Keeping the time very consistent is the key to making these patterns practical. In most musical settings, the kick doesn't play groups of four notes. It is still important to gain this facility since often the kick may have to play three- or four-note phrases leading out of fills to accent the downbeat of the next measure. There is only one version of the four-note groups since the hands and feet are playing an even amount of notes in the measure.

DEVELOPMENTAL IDEA

The four-note groups are the most difficult, especially on the kick drum. As in three-notes groups, a slight crescendo leading to the fourth note will help the musicality of the phrase. Think about each four-note phrase always building to the heavily accented fourth note. The discussion on kick drum foot technique in *The Drum Set Crash Course* video will help take some of the mystery out of multiple-note kick drum patterns.

EXERCISE TRACK

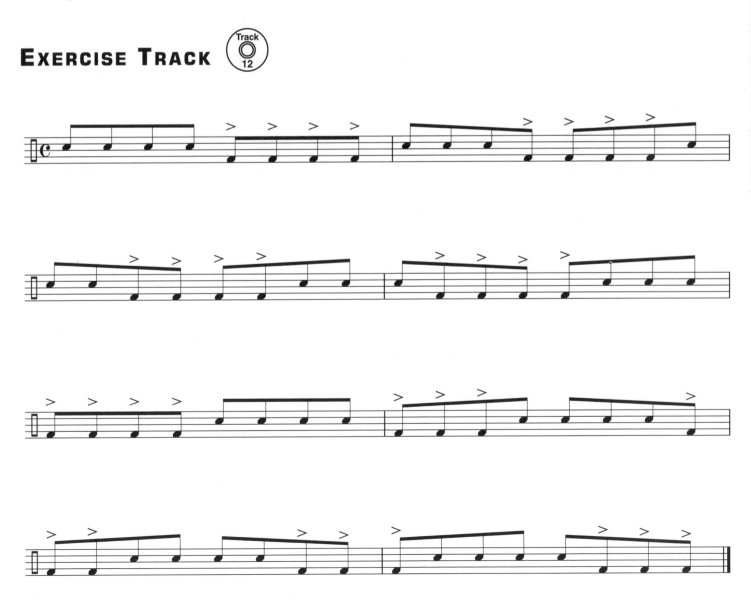

This is the first of the 32-bar exercises. These combination exercises are designed to present as many combinations of one, two, three, and four notes in continuous measures as possible. Really try to lock in with the click and the band on the exercise play-along tracks. It will also help to count/sing through the measures so you don't get lost in the time. Although it is possible to put only one tempo of play-along on the accompanying CD, it is very important to practice all of the exercises at many tempo ranges (60–180 B.P.M.).

EXERCISE TRACK

LINEAR MIX OF STRAIGHT EIGHTH-NOTE PLAY-ALONG

EXERCISE TRACK (Track 15) & (Track 16)

ROC-A-LONG

By RUSS MILLER, GANNIN ARNOLD
and JONATHAN AHRENS

Two-Limb Independence
Linear Exercises, Eighth-Note Triplets
Twelve Subdivisions

The second concept in the two-limb or linear studies is the ability to play eighth-note triplets. Eighth-note triplets are a basic note flow that subdivides the measure into 12 equal parts. For this section of the book, a 12/8 time signature will be used. 12/8 is very similar to a 4/4 time signature. Reading eighth-note triplets is much easier in a 12/8 time signature because there does not need to be triplet bars around each figure. These markings sometimes make it slightly harder to read triplet figures and can be a bit confusing. From a technical standpoint, three-note figures per beat in 12/8 are not triplets. Because of the 12/8 time signature, the beats are usually always already divided into three parts. The three-note figures in 12/8 feel and are played exactly the same as eighth-note triplets in 4/4, so 12/8 is used here for the ease of reading. This book will refer to each of these as eighth-note triplets for ease of understanding and recognition. A measure full of eighth-note triplets in 4/4 looks like this:

A measure of 12/8 with three-note subdivisions looks like this:

Eighth-note triplets are the foundation for many styles of music. Blues, jazz, Afro-Cuban 6/8 styles, pop shuffles, and others are all based around eighth-note triplets. The first step is to practice playing 12 notes evenly spaced in a measure. Make sure to use a metronome set to play eighth-note triplets (1/12th) subdivisions. Use just one hand at first, and then switch to the opposite hand. Playing these triplets with an alternating sticking is very important. Because of the odd number of notes in one beat, the leading hand will switch back and forth as you play through the measure. This helps to work out an ambidextrous facility.

After playing the basic triplet note flow at a range of 60–180 B.P.M., it is time to start using interplay of the kick and hands in an eighth-note triplet flow.

Here is the first exercise to incorporate the kick drum into eight-note triplets. The play-along track demonstrates a basic blues music form in which the bass guitar is laying down a quarter-note feel. It is the drum set player's job to create the strong and consistent eighth-note triplet pulse. Really listen to the click on the play-along track. The first note of each of the three-note groups must line up perfectly with the click at the downbeat of each beat. This is one of the keys to getting the even spacing of the 12 notes in each measure.

DEVELOPMENTAL IDEA

Eighth-note triplets have a very distinct tension to their sound. This happens because they are based on an odd number of notes in one beat. Along with standard counting techniques (1-da-da, 2-da-da or 1-trip-let , 2-trip-let), the focus toward each of the downbeats is crucial. This forces the player to execute the triplet at an even spacing in each beat. The tendency is to rush the kick drum notes into the flow of time. Counting and singing the time through the voicing (hand to kick) transition is very important.

EXERCISE TRACK (Track 17) & (Track 21)

This exercise is purely for the development of your kick drum foot. This is probably not going to come up in many practical playing circumstances; however, the ability to feel and execute the eight-note triplet note flow with your kick drum foot is very important. You may need to work for awhile with just the metronome at slower tempos before playing the exercise track, which is fine because there is a very important physical development that has to happen in building drum set facility. Exercises like these help build the muscles used to play certain figures. They will have a drastic effect on how confidently you execute eighth-note triplets with your foot in the future.

EXERCISE TRACK Track 17 & Track 21

This is the introduction of playing two-note groups in a triplet-note flow. Remember that it is very common to "rush" two-note figures played with the same limb. In the beginning, counting/singing this note flow will help your execution greatly.

DEVELOPMENTAL IDEA

Using a slightly stronger accent on the second note of the two-note group will help prevent you from rushing the figure. Give the second note its full value in time. It becomes extremely important to remain very consistent at medium tempos, since it is much harder to play at medium tempos than at fast tempos. Medium tempos require the player to control the body's natural desire to play figures faster in order to get through them.

EXERCISE TRACK

This is the foot development exercise using two-note groups in each measure. Remember to alternate the leading hand for the two-note figures. It is sometimes more difficult to have interplay between the kick drum foot and your opposite leading hand (left hand for right-handers and right hand for the southpaws!).

EXERCISE TRACK Track 23

The introduction of the three-note phrase into the triplet flow creates some very interesting rhythmic figures. Because of the odd number of notes in each beat, there will be groups of four, five, and seven phrased in three. These are some very advanced techniques that we end up playing through our thorough exploration of these basic triplet concepts. At quicker tempos, these are great kick drum exercises. The hint to use the slight crescendo really helps in the development of these figures. Also, a heavier accent on the third note of each group makes it easier to play. Alternate the leading hands and try to count/sing through the transition from foot to hands.

EXERCISE TRACK

Track 25

Again, purely for foot development, the three-note groups leading with the foot are quite challenging. Don't get frustrated if the play-along track is at a tempo a little too quick to play at the start. Work with the metronome at first. A great regiment to work on is playing the figures at one B.P.M. marking for ten minutes each. Then, add two metronome markings at a time until the play-along tempo is reached. It is probably not necessary to go beyond the tempo of the play-along track for an exercise such as this. On the other hand, working on this at quicker tempos could make the baddest kick foot that ever lived!

EXERCISE TRACK (Track 25)

The concept of four-note groups per measure can be very difficult to grasp at first. The groups of four notes phrased within the triplet flow create some interesting odd-phrased figures. Use the slight crescendo technique for the kick figures, as well as accenting the last note in the group. Counting/singing the triplet pulse will definitely be a must at first. This is a great approach to learn early on in drum set studies. This will open up the understanding of different phrasing in note flows and what is possible in basic hand-to-foot playing. Understanding this approach is important so that when additional independence comes into play (in the next section of the book), the odd phrases won't cause more confusion than necessary.

DEVELOPMENTAL IDEA

One of the most helpful hints when attempting to play this exercise is to count/sing the triplet note flow. Sometimes the voicing (snare, kick, cymbals, and so on) of the notes being played plays havoc with the ear's understanding of the figures being played. The interplay between the kick and hands can make basic figures sound more difficult. Concentrating the basic flow of notes going by (triplets in this case) is needed to execute this exercise with confidence.

EXERCISE TRACK

Track 27

The kick drum leading version of the four-note group exercise is definitely challenging. Keep the focus on the consistency of the notes and the technique with the foot. As mentioned before, the kick drum foot technique discussion in *The Drum Set Crash Course* video is a good study in the execution of figures such as these. Remember to lead with each hand for the four-note groups in each measure.

EXERCISE TRACK

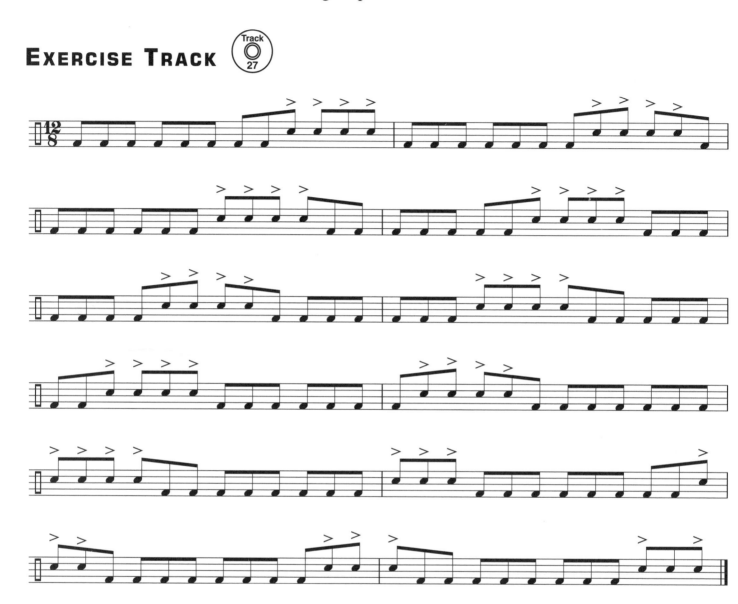

The 32-bar exercise for eight-note triplets is actually 36 bars long. This is because the play-along is in a traditional 12-bar blues song form. The horn section is playing the combination figures, so the key is to really lock in with the band. Try to listen for how the horns articulate (add color to) the various figures. Some notes are longer, shorter, higher, or lower. Think about what the drum set could do to help accentuate the articulations of the horn section. What instruments should be used to help accentuate short notes? Or long notes? This understanding of what is going on in the rest of the band will be extremely important in the perception of playing music in the future. Keep in mind that it is not necessary at this stage of development to play the hand figures on only one instrument. Although there are instruments mixed into the exercise track to complete the drum set parts, moving some voicings around while working on this exercise can create some interesting musical ideas.

LINEAR MIX OF EIGHTH-NOTE TRIPLET PLAY-ALONG

EXERCISE TRACK Track 30 & Track 31

BIMINI

By RIQUE PANTOJA

Two-Limb Independence
Linear Exercises, Sixteenth Notes
Sixteenth subdivisions

The third main note flow covered in here in sixteenth notes. A measure is now divided into sixteen equal subdivisions. Use basic counting methods for sixteenths (1-e-and-ah) to help feel the positions of the various figures. Remember that several different stickings can be used to play through the snare drum leading patterns. Sticking studies are a whole other book in itself, so those variations will not be covered here. I recommend studying with a private instructor snare drum rudiment and sticking studies books. Basic variations such as R R R R / L L L L / R L R L / L R L R are a good starting place. The concept of this chapter is the same as the previous ones.

Developmental Idea

The bass guitar on the exercise play-along track is playing a sixteenth-note flow. This is a good focal point to listen to. Try to lock in exactly with the bass player on the track. The concept of really listening to other players in the band and locking in with them is a crucial part of playing music. It is great to start this approach early in the study of this instrument. One of the most common tendencies when playing these exercises is to slow down in the transition from the kick drum to the snare drum. The flow of notes must sound very consistent even if different limbs are playing amongst the figures. Since the kick drum is sort of "waiting around" to play, while working on the snare drum leading exercises, the tendency is for the kick to enter late. Counting/singing the time and flow of notes will help center the time mentally. This will force the limbs to play in time. It is not common to slow down while verbally counting or singing. The human mind knows what these flows of notes are supposed to sound like. The physical challenges are what cause the errors in the performances. These sixteenth-note exercises are easier to keep time than subdivisions that have less notes per bar. The more subdivisions in a measure, the less space there is to make mistakes. This book will only break down the measure as far as sixteenth notes. Another common subdivision is sextuplets (24 subdivisions in a measure), which will not be covered in this edition. The independence required for sextuplets is very similar to eight-note triplets, just in double-time. The amount of facility built by covering the various subdivisions in this edition will more than prepare the body for the physical challenges of practical playing circumstances.

Two-Limb Independence/Linear Sixteenth-Note One-Note Groups

Exercise Track  **&**

Snare Drum Lead

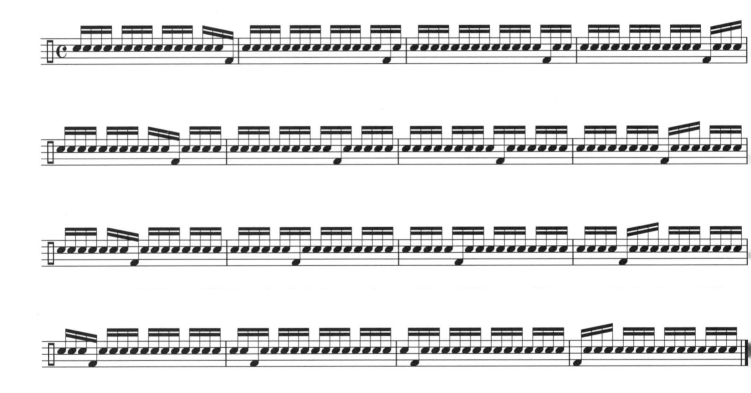

TWO-LIMB INDEPENDENCE/LINEAR SIXTEENTH-NOTE ONE-NOTE GROUPS

EXERCISE TRACK  **&**

Obvious by the look of this exercise, this kick drum leading sixteenth exercise is purely for the development of the kick foot. It will also help with the transitions from hand to foot.

Kick Drum Lead

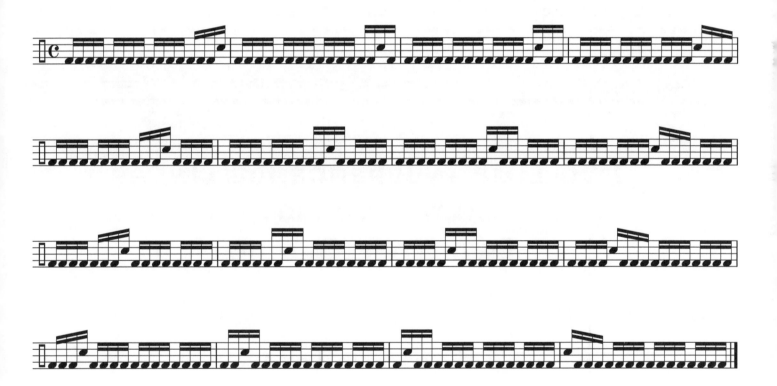

Two-Limb Independence/Linear Sixteenth-Note Two-Note Groups

Snare Drum Lead

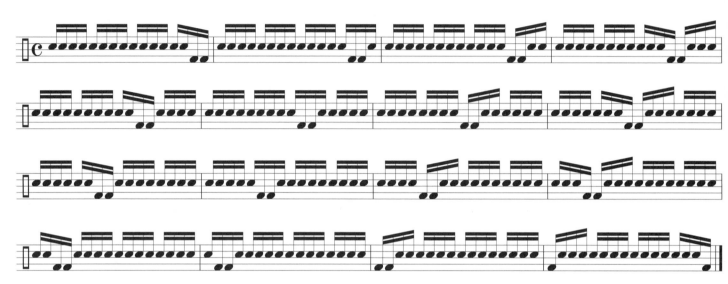

Two-Limb Independence/Linear Sixteenth-Note Two-Note Groups

Kick Drum Lead

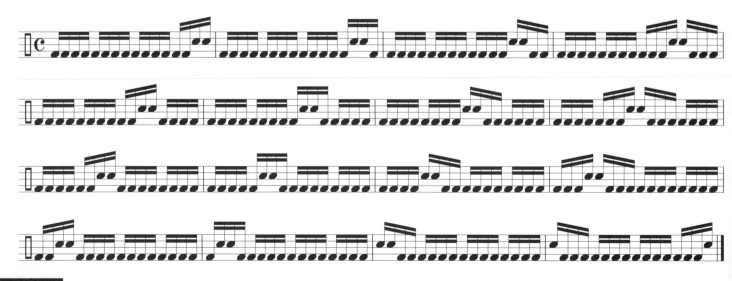

Two-Limb Independence/Linear Sixteenth-Note Three-Note Groups

EXERCISE TRACK

DEVELOPMENTAL IDEA

When working on this three-note group version of the linear sixteenth-notes, remember to use the crescendo leading to the third note. As in the earlier chapters, this approach will make the figures sound more musical. This concept in characterizing (known as articulating) the note figures will become extremely important as the progression on the drum set develops.

Snare Drum Lead

Two-Limb Independence/Linear Sixteenth-Note Three-Note Groups

Exercise Track

Developmental Idea 💡

Work with a metronome with this kick drum development exercise. Start at about 60 B.P.M. and gradually work up to the tempo of the play-along track. This will definitely develop the kick foot, but this is also for working on the interaction of kick and snare. This exercise forces the placement of snare notes around kick drum phrases. This will be a great help later when working through various combination figures in full compositions.

Kick Drum Lead

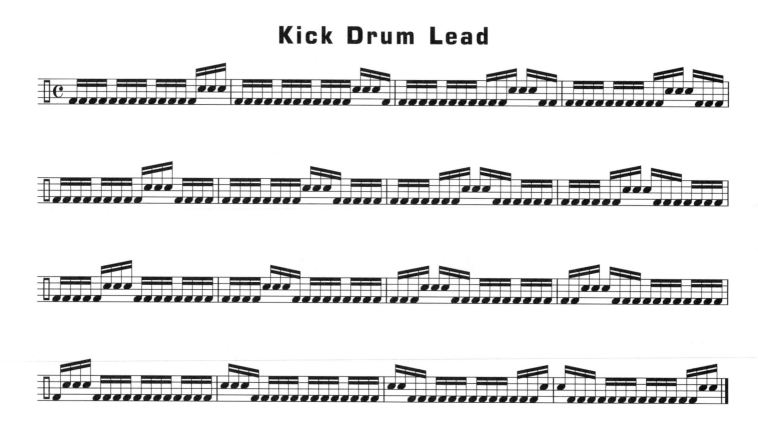

Two-Limb Independence/Linear Sixteenth-Note Four-Note Groups

Exercise Track Track 42

Snare Drum Lead

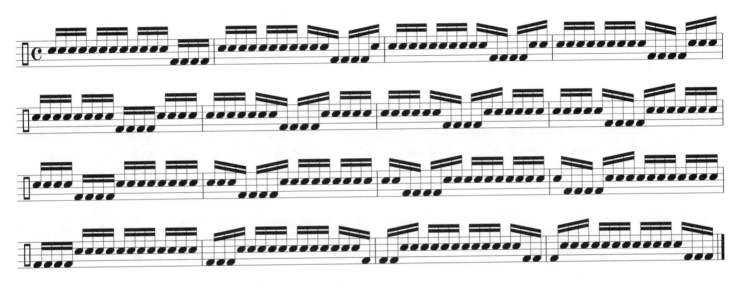

Two-Limb Independence/Linear Sixteenth-Note Four-Note Groups

Exercise Track Track 42

Kick Drum Lead

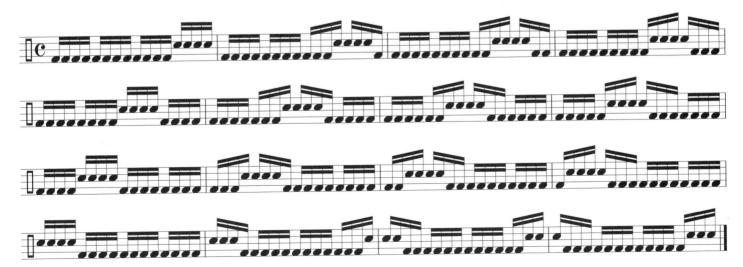

Two-Limb Linear Independence Sixteenth-Note 32-Bar Combination Exercise

This is the 32-bar combination exercise for linear sixteenth notes. The bass guitar on the play-along track is playing a definite sixteenth-note flow. Focus on this flow in order to lock into the time. The snare plays the consistent sixteenth notes, and the kick will hit the figures with the percussion. Try to line up exactly with the percussion figures as they are played.

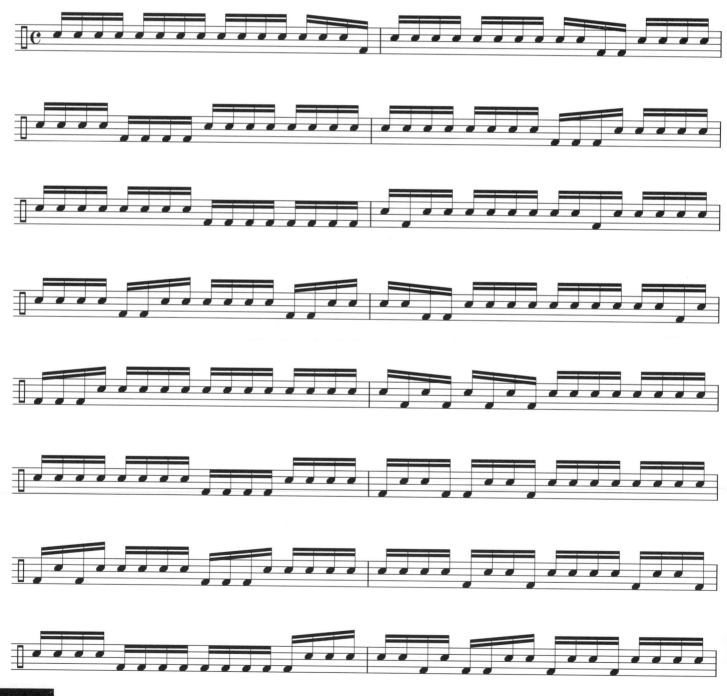

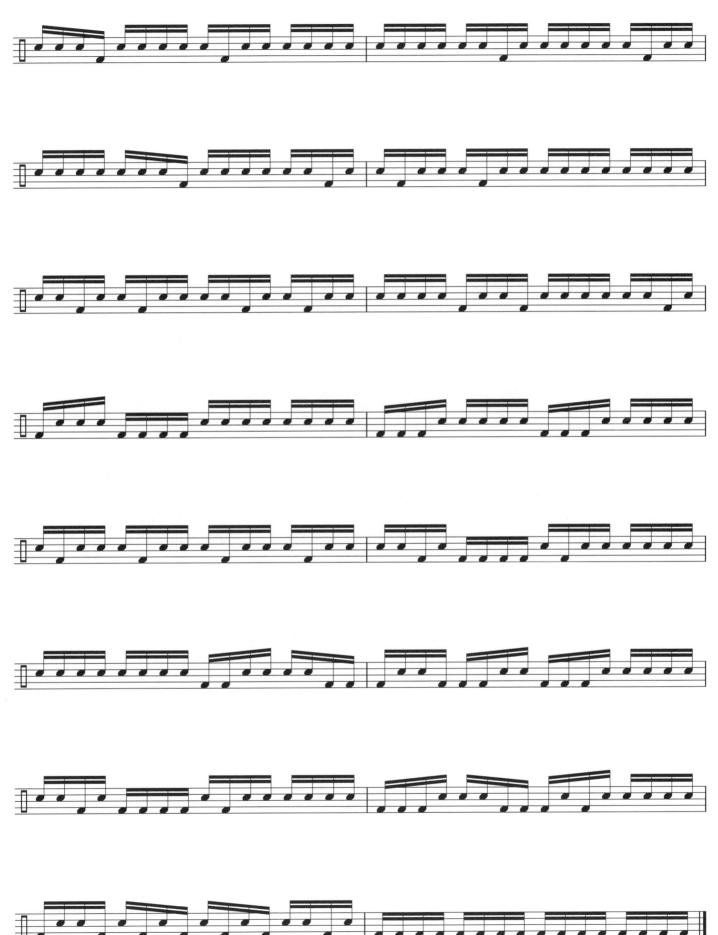

SYSTEM SCRATCH PAD

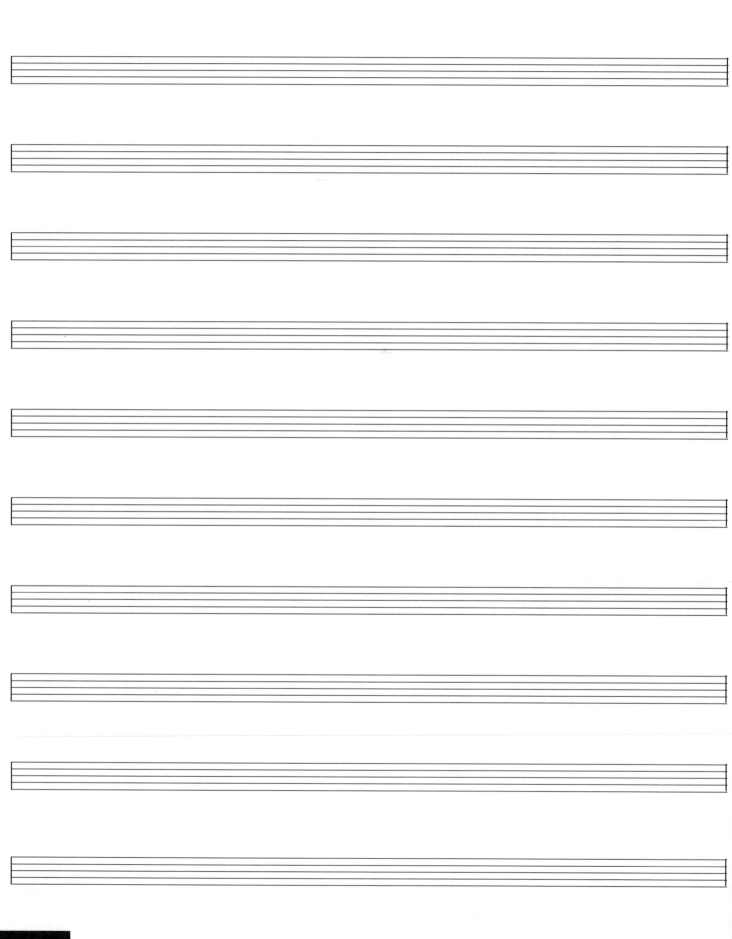

LINEAR MIX OF SIXTEENTH-NOTE PLAY-ALONG

EXERCISE TRACK **&**

BRINCADEIRA

By RIQUE PANTOJA

CHAPTER TWO
Two-Limb Independence
Straight-Eighth Notes

Now that the facility to play the basic flows of notes has been developed, it's time to start adding the challenge of multi-limb independence. The term "two-limb independence" means that two limbs of the body are playing completely different rhythms at the same time. The exercises in the following section of study will incorporate the riding hand playing on the closed hi-hat while the snare hand and kick foot play various figures between them. Not every pattern or groove involves playing patterns that don't relate to each other at all; in fact, many will interact quite a bit. Development of a true independence facility does involve playing patterns that are sometimes completely separate in rhythmic interaction. The following is an example of a basic two-limb exercise written out with the patterns put together. This combination is Hand Pattern #1 and the first measure of the first exercise written together.

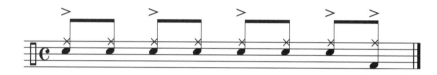

It is easy to see the interaction of the various rhythms when you notate the exercise in this manner. The systems in the independence chapters of this book are written with each limb grouped separately for ease of choosing many combinations. A basic example of choosing limb patterns and combining them is written above. Two-limb independence studies require choosing one of the right-hand patterns to play while reading the written linear exercises. I use the term "line-up" to describe two limbs playing notes at exactly the same time. A "flamming" effect can happen if the notes are played at slightly different times. A "flam" refers to the rudiment when one note hits just before the other (a grace note). When working on the rudiments, this is a desired effect at times. It is not desired when working on independence studies. When too much flamming occurs, the patterns will sound sloppy and will not sound musical.

The following page starts the first two-limb system in straight eighth notes. For all of the independence systems from this chapter forward, select a riding hand pattern and then play through each of the exercises. Each exercise will now have four different possibilities of riding hand patterns. Remember to focus on the limbs "lining up" so the patterns will sound musical.

Two-Limb Independence
Straight-Eighth Notes
One-Note Groups

System Combination Example:
• Riding Hand Pattern #1
• One-Note Group Measure #1

Riding Hand Patterns

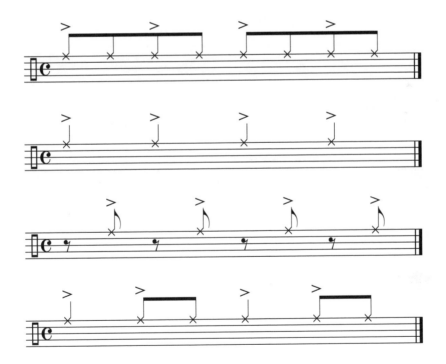

STRAIGHT-EIGHTH NOTES WITH
ONE-NOTE GROUPS
SNARE DRUM LEAD

EXERCISE TRACK (Track 3) & (Track 6)

KICK DRUM LEAD

Two-Limb Independence
Straight-Eighth Notes
Two-Note Groups

The same concept applies to the two-note systems as to the one-note systems played previously. Remember my hint of accenting the second note more than the first to give the note its proper value. One common habit in multiple-limb independence studies is subconsciously allowing all of the limbs to follow each other's accents and other articulations. Each limb has its own dynamics and character. Just because your right hand is accenting a note doesn't mean your right foot should as well! This is where the challenge of separating the limbs comes into play.

Riding Hand Patterns

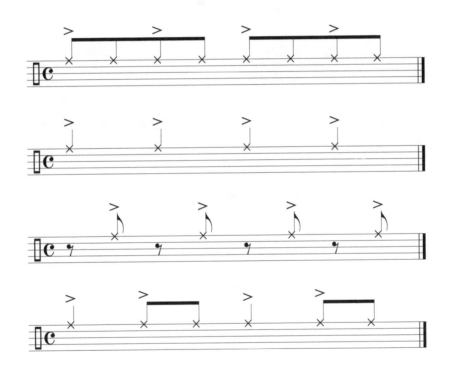

STRAIGHT-EIGHTH NOTES WITH TWO-NOTE GROUPS
SNARE DRUM LEAD

EXERCISE TRACK (Track 8)

KICK DRUM LEAD

TWO-LIMB INDEPENDENCE
STRAIGHT-EIGHTH NOTES
THREE-NOTE GROUPS

Don't forget some of the hints on playing three-note groups discussed in the previous chapters. Keep in mind that it is important to work with the metronome through different B.P.M. ranges. Work up to and past the play-along track's tempo. Each of these systems will build different facilities for different musical situations.

RIDING HAND PATTERNS

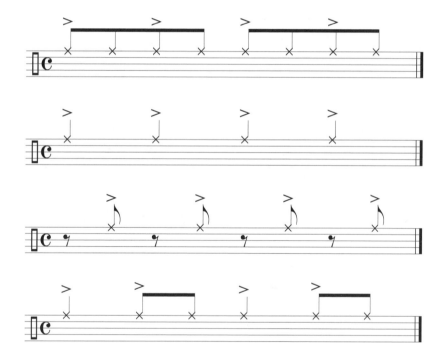

STRAIGHT-EIGHTH NOTES WITH THREE-NOTE GROUPS

SNARE DRUM LEAD

KICK DRUM LEAD

TWO-LIMB INDEPENDENCE
STRAIGHT-EIGHTH NOTES
FOUR-NOTE GROUPS

The four-note groups work the kick and snare limbs evenly. There is no need to have a snare lead version and then a kick lead version. Use the crescendo leading to the last note in the four-note group to make the figures more musical. This will also make it easier to execute.

EXERCISE TRACK (Track 12)

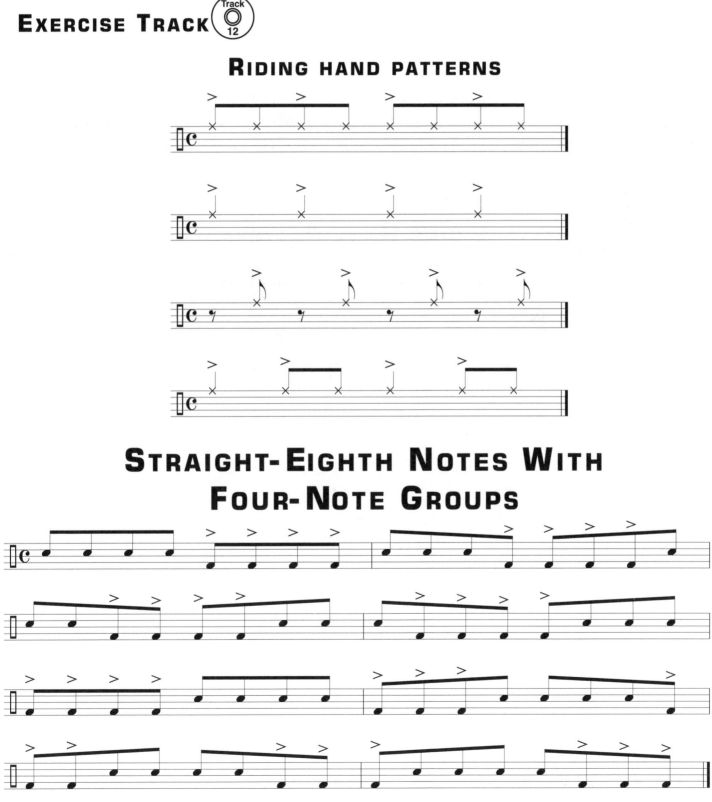

RIDING HAND PATTERNS

STRAIGHT-EIGHTH NOTES WITH
FOUR-NOTE GROUPS

TWO-LIMB INDEPENDENCE
STRAIGHT-EIGHTH NOTES
32-BAR COMBINATION EXERCISE

EXERCISE TRACK

The 32-bar exercise will test the ability to execute multiple-note groupings in each measure. Pick one of the riding hand patterns and play through the entire exercise. Then try the remaining patterns to create different combinations for the exercise.

RIDING HAND PATTERNS

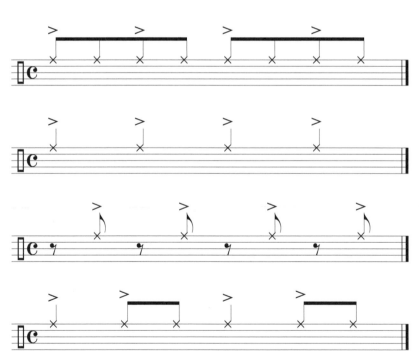

STRAIGHT-EIGHTH NOTE 32-BAR COMBINATION EXERCISE

SYSTEM SCRATCH PAD

Two-Limb Mix of Eighth-Note Play-Along

EXERCISE TRACK **&**

ROC-A-LONG

By RUSS MILLER, GANNIN ARNOLD
and JONATHAN AHRENS

TWO-LIMB INDEPENDENCE
EIGHTH-NOTE TRIPLETS
TWELVE SUBDIVISIONS

The eighth-note triplet studies of two-limb independence are very similar to the straight eighth-note study. As in the linear triplet studies, the odd number of notes per beat will cause the leading hand to switch back and forth. This is slightly more challenging because the independence movements are changing every time the lead hand changes. Whenever a consistent flow of triplets is played, this will occur. Working with a metronome while playing through these exercises (at various B.P.M.s) will slowly develop a confidence in playing triplet flows. Work up to and beyond the play-along's tempo. This is recommended for every system in *Transitions*. Here is an example of one of the triplet exercises assembled. This is Riding Hand Pattern #1 with the first measure of the one-note group exercise:

Again, the horn section will be playing all of the note groupings on the play-along track. Listen for how they articulate the various patterns. Keep in mind, in a practical situation, that the drum kit will need to articulate these phrases in a similar manner (long/short and high/low notes). This is why the play-along exercise tracks are so important. Generally, playing these "musical" patterns and phrases is not usually approached until much later in a student's studies. With this book, an understanding of listening and reacting to musical phrases is approached from the start of your studies. We are musicians who play drums, not drummers who hang out with musicians!

TWO-LIMB INDEPENDENCE
EIGHTH-NOTE TRIPLETS
ONE-NOTE GROUPS

     As in the linear eighth-note triplet studies, this system is in a 12/8 time signature. This is mainly for ease of reading. The measures are phrased in four-beat phrases, like a measure of 4/4. The dotted quarter notes in 12/8 feel like quarter notes in 4/4. Don't allow this time signature change to confuse you. It is easier to read in 12/8 than in 4/4 with triplet bars placed around phrases. The riding hand patterns for the triplet exercises are notated below. Choose one of these hand patterns and play through the system. Then go back and use each one of them until the system has been conquered using all of the hand patterns.

RIDING HAND PATTERNS

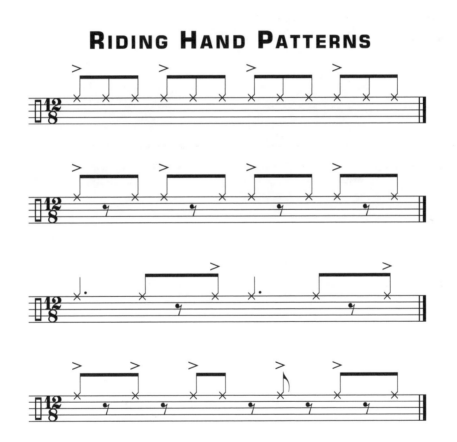

EIGHTH-NOTE TRIPLET PATTERNS WITH ONE-NOTE GROUPS
SNARE DRUM LEAD

EXERCISE TRACK (Track 18) & (Track 21)

TWO-LIMB INDEPENDENCE
EIGHTH-NOTE TRIPLETS
ONE-NOTE GROUPS

EXERCISE TRACK (Track 18) & (Track 21)

RIDING HAND PATTERNS

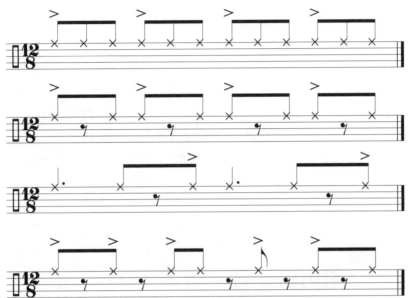

EIGHTH-NOTE TRIPLET PATTERNS WITH
ONE-NOTE GROUPS
KICK DRUM LEAD

TWO-LIMB INDEPENDENCE
TWO-NOTE GROUPS

EXERCISE TRACK

Here is the two-note group exercise for eighth-note triplets. The hints about accenting the second note apply here as well. For the kick drum exercise, working up to the speed of the play-along may be difficult. Don't get frustrated; this is simply a physical exercise to develop foot control and facility. Again, refer to the foot technique discussion on *The Drum Set Crash Course* video for some technical hints.

RIDING HAND PATTERNS

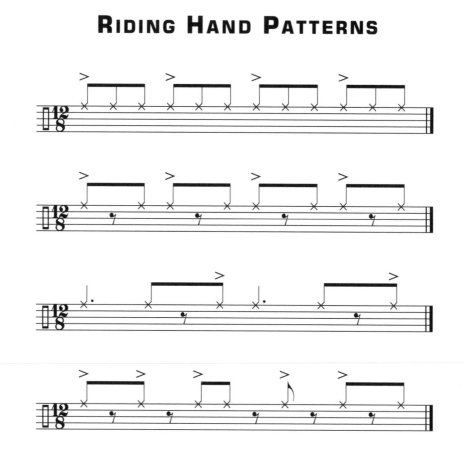

EIGHTH-NOTE TRIPLET PATTERNS WITH TWO-NOTE GROUPS
SNARE DRUM LEAD

EIGHTH-NOTE TRIPLET PATTERNS WITH TWO-NOTE GROUPS
KICK DRUM LEAD

EXERCISE TRACK (Track 23)

RIDING HAND PATTERNS

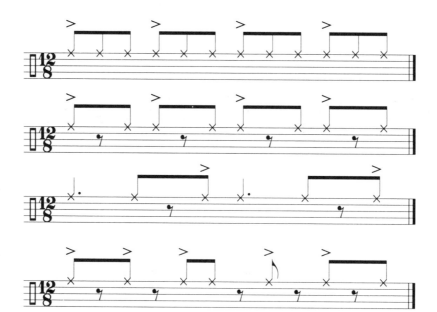

TWO-LIMB INDEPENDENCE
THREE-NOTE GROUPS

EXERCISE TRACK

    The three-note groups exercise is similar to the previous three-note exercises. The slight crescendo leading to the third note of the accented group will help. Keep in mind that these figures are all played by the horn section just as they will be in a practical musical setting. The concept is the same but intensified for quick development purposes. By practicing only rhythmic figures played by instruments in whole compositions, it will take a lot of searching through albums to find every possible combination of hits in a full measure. *Transitions* mirrors what is required to play some of these figures while keeping time in a practical composition style setting. But these exercises cover every possible combination of these multi-group figures in a 12-bar exercise. Have fun!

RIDING HAND PATTERNS

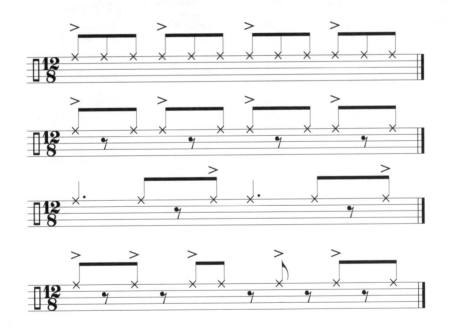

Eighth-Note Triplet Patterns With Three-Note Groups
Snare Drum Lead

EIGHTH-NOTE TRIPLET PATTERNS WITH THREE-NOTE GROUPS
KICK DRUM LEAD

EXERCISE TRACK

RIDING HAND PATTERNS

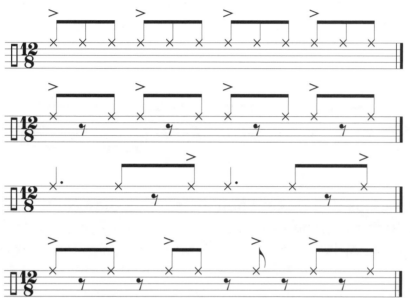

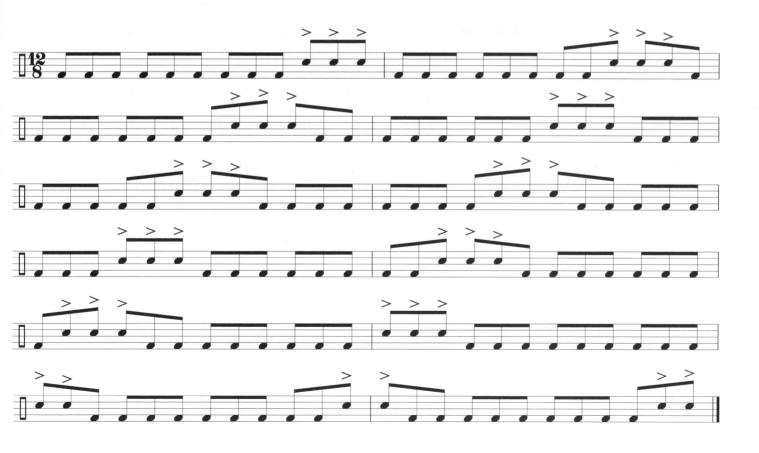

TWO-LIMB INDEPENDENCE
FOUR-NOTE GROUPS

EXERCISE TRACK

The four-note group exercise uses the same approach as one-, two-, and three-note groups. Choose one of the riding hand patterns and play through each of the 12-bar exercises. Here is an example of Riding Hand Pattern #3 with the first bar of the snare drum lead exercise.

If the combinations that occur when assembling these system exercises start to get confusing, use the System Scratch Pad page at the end of these exercises. This blank sheet of manuscript paper is for use in assembling the combinations on paper so they may be approached very slowly. Remember, though, that the idea of *Transitions* is not to approach the drum set from this standpoint. The process of thinking about these combinations in how the limbs relate to each other first is an incorrect method of study. The idea is to use the concept of having the facility to play all of these band figures while keeping time with any riding pattern chosen. The study of independence should not become a method of learning how notes fall on top of each other and slowly assembling specific patterns. If this is the case, only the ability to execute those specific combinations of patterns in a practical setting will have been gained. This leads to a drummer forcing a "grab bag" of tricks into a musical composition. Let the music determine what it wants from the drum set. Don't force drum playing into music! There is a big difference between a great drummer and a great musician who plays drums!

RIDING PATTERNS

These are the four riding patterns for four-note groups.

EIGHTH-NOTE TRIPLET PATTERNS WITH FOUR-NOTE GROUPS
SNARE DRUM LEAD

EXERCISE TRACK (Track 27)

EIGHTH-NOTE TRIPLET PATTERNS WITH
FOUR-NOTE GROUPS
KICK DRUM LEAD

EXERCISE TRACK

TWO-LIMB 36-BAR COMBINATION EXERCISE

EXERCISE TRACK (Track 29)

The 36-bar combination exercise for two-limb independence is similar to the linear combination exercise. This next challenge level is playing through this exercise with each of the riding hand patterns. As before, select one of the riding hand patterns and play with the play-along track through the entire exercise. This is designed to involve combinations of one-, two-, three, and four-note groups in a measure. The horn section is playing unison with the written figures. Again, think about the articulations of the horns. This ability to recognize other instruments' articulations will prove valuable in the next section of this book and throughout any other musical experiences.

RIDING HAND PATTERNS

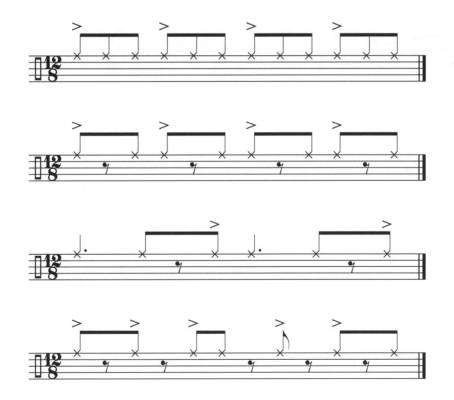

Two-Limb 36-Bar Combination Exercise
Eighth-Note Triplets

EXERCISE TRACK

Two-Limb 36-Bar Combination Exercise
Eighth-Note Triplets, continued

SYSTEM SCRATCH PAD

TWO-LIMB MIX OF EIGHTH-NOTE TRIPLET PLAY-ALONG

EXERCISE TRACK **&**

BIMINI

By RIQUE PANTOJA

TWO-LIMB INDEPENDENCE
SIXTEENTH NOTES
ONE-NOTE GROUPS

DEVELOPMENTAL IDEA

The following riding patterns are for use with the sixteenth-note two-limb exercises. First, practice just the riding hand patterns with the snare drum playing a straight sixteenth note flow. Focus on each of the riding hand notes lining up with the sixteenth-note pulse in the snare hand. It will be very apparent when the notes are not happening exactly together. This is a great exercise to start with. As the exercises progress, the figures will become harder as more independence is added. If the concept of really locking in with your limbs is developed, it will carry on through the more difficult physical challenges to come.

RIDING HAND PATTERNS

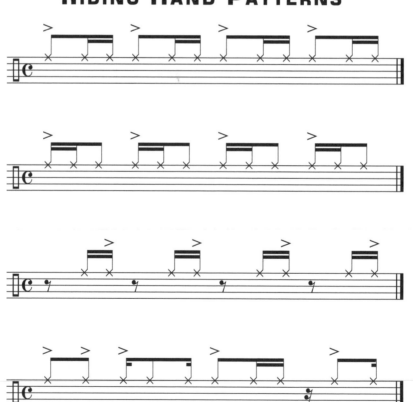

Two-Limb Independence
Sixteenth-Notes
One-Note Groups

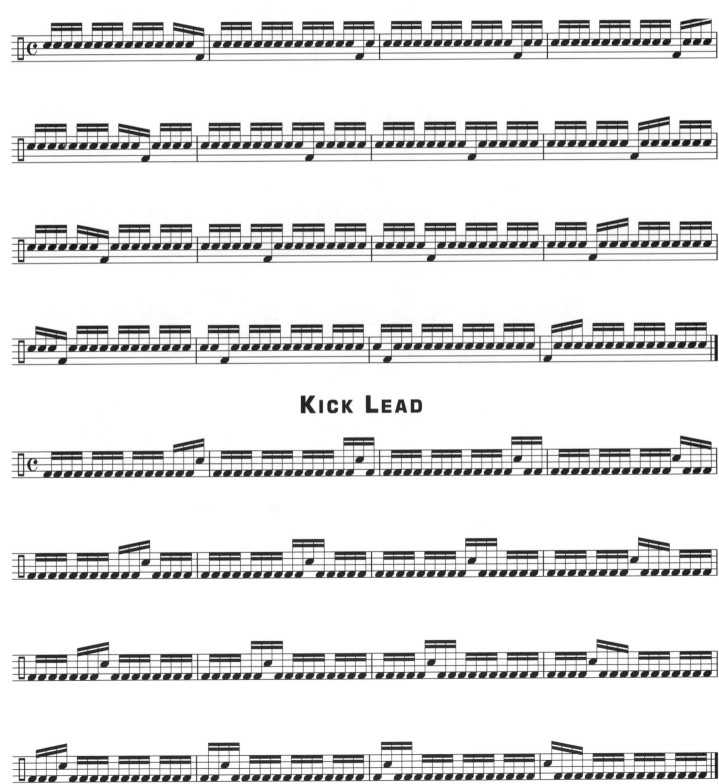

TWO-LIMB INDEPENDENCE
SIXTEENTH NOTES
TWO-NOTE GROUPS

DEVELOPMENTAL IDEA

The most common tendency for these exercises is to rush the groups of two-note figures. Listen and focus on the bass line for the time. Leave the correct amount of space between the groups of two notes.

RIDING HAND PATTERNS

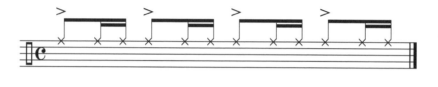

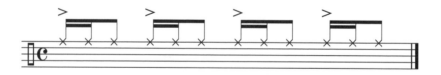

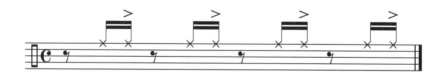

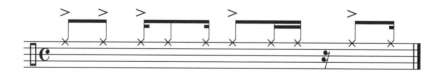

Two-Limb Independence
Two-Note Groups
Snare Lead

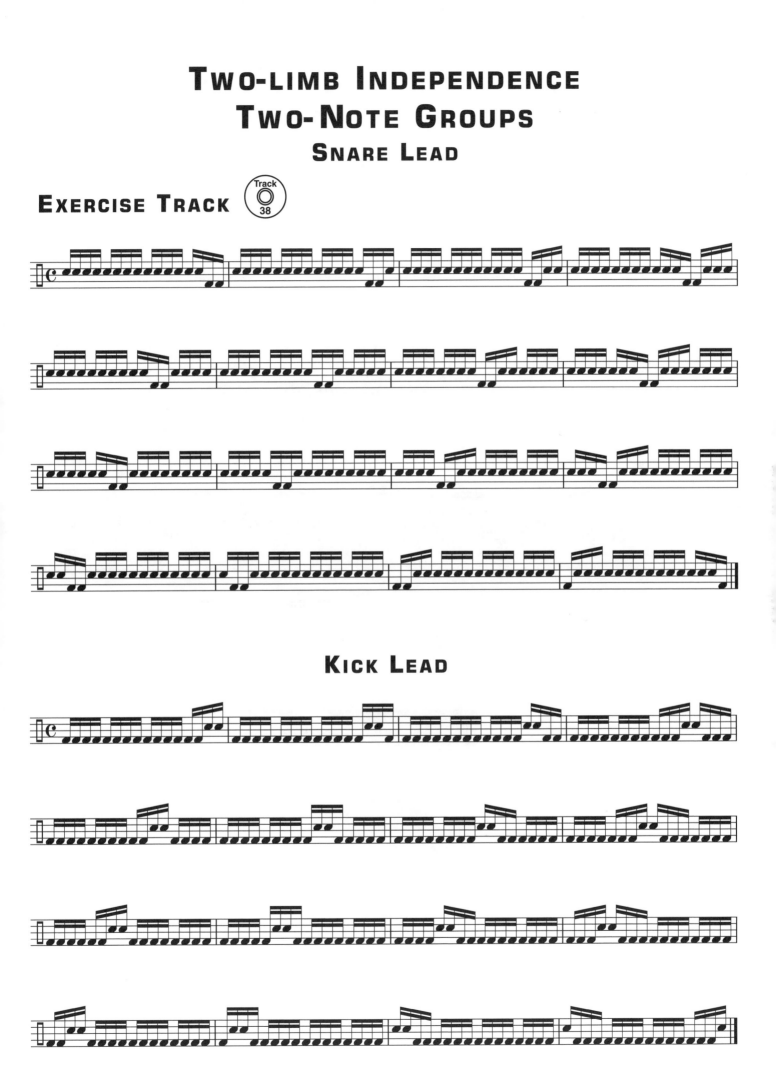

Kick Lead

TWO-LIMB INDEPENDENCE
SIXTEENTH-NOTES
THREE-NOTE GROUPS

RIDING HAND PATTERNS

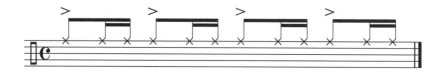

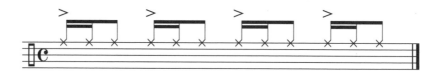

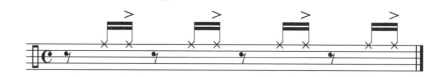

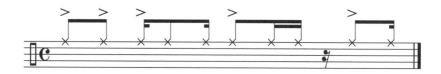

Russ performing at 2001 Grammys

Two-Limb Independence
Three-Note Groups

Exercise Track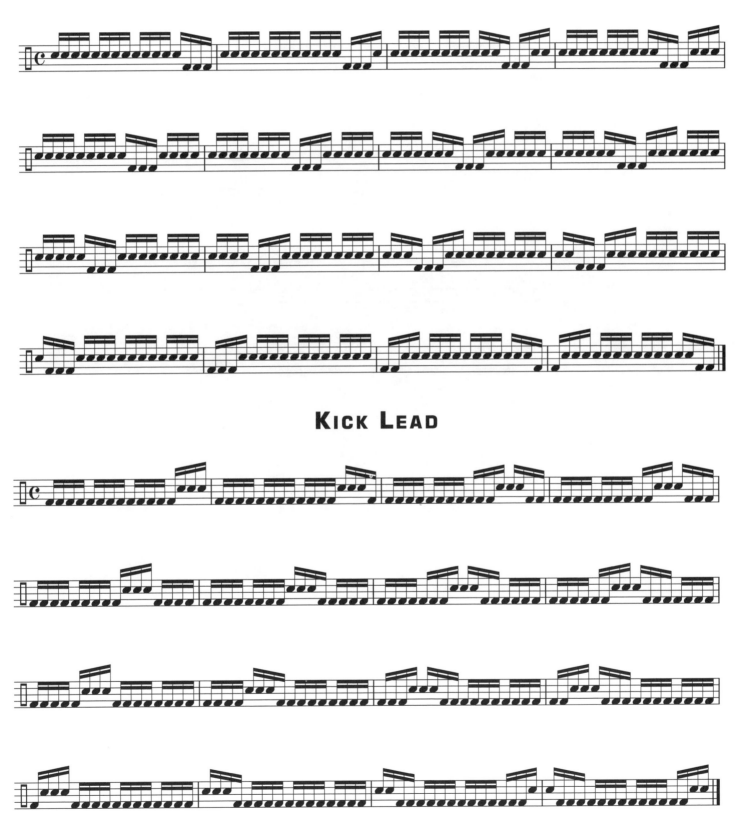

Track
40

Snare Lead

Kick Lead

Two-Limb Independence
Sixteenth Notes
Four-Note Groups

Riding Hand Patterns

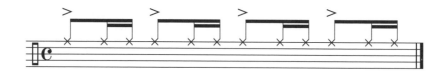

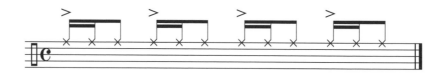

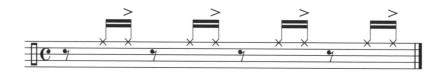

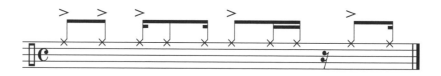

TWO-LIMB INDEPENDENCE
FOUR-NOTE GROUPS

SNARE LEAD

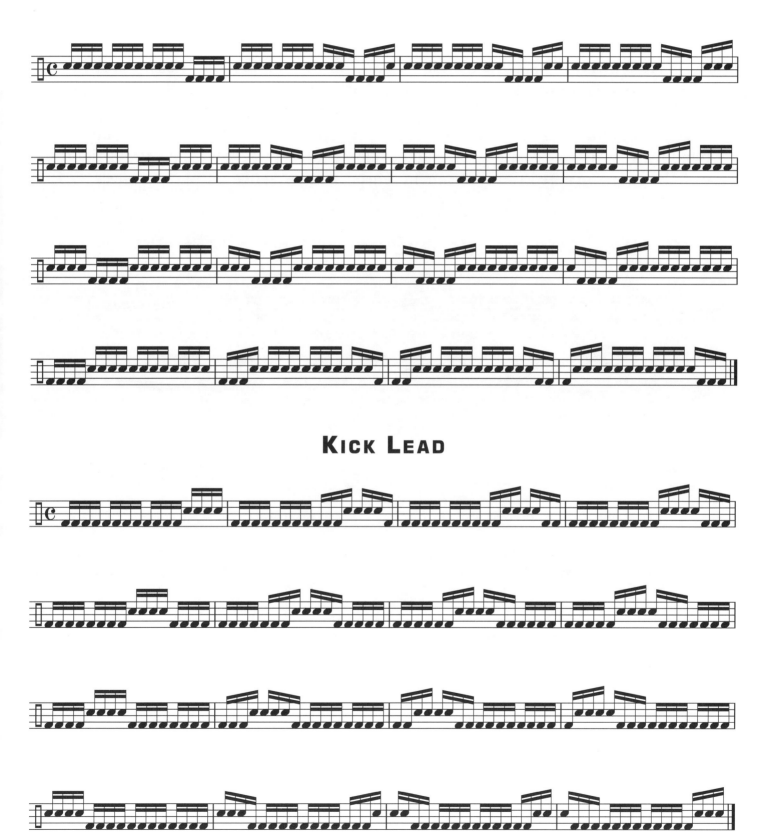

KICK LEAD

Two-Limb Independence Sixteenth-Note 32-Bar Combination Exercise

Exercise Track

Here is the 32-bar combination exercise for two-limb independence involving sixteenth notes. This exercise works the interplay between snare and kick drum. The percussion is playing the various figures that are voiced onto the kick drum throughout the exercise. Another variation of this exercise is to start the kick drum first and hit the band figures with the snare (great foot development!). Try to play the various figures exactly when the percussion plays them. This is great practice for playing music.

*Choose Any of the Previous Riding Hand Patterns

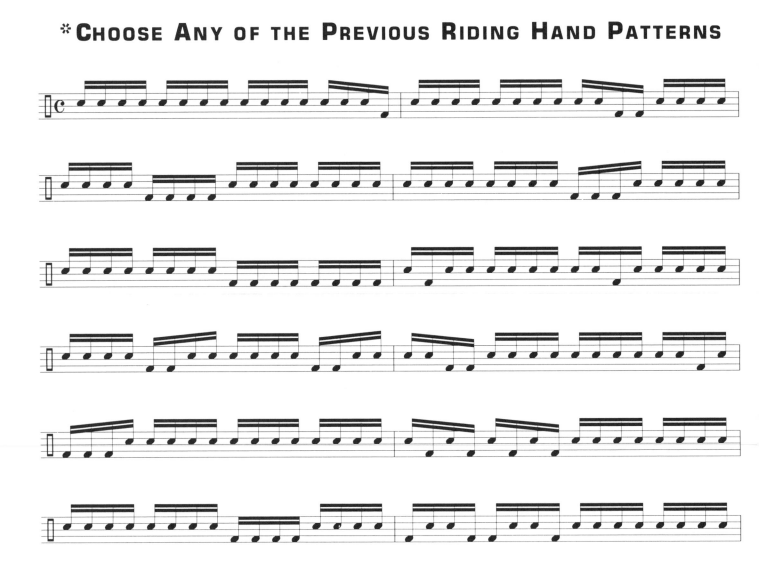

Two-Limb Independence Sixteenth-Notes
32-Bar Combination Exercise, continued

SYSTEM SCRATCH PAD

Two-Limb Mix of Sixteenth-Note Play-Along

EXERCISE TRACK Track 45 & Track 46

BRINCADEIRA

By RIQUE PANTOJA

SYSTEM SCRATCH PAD

CHAPTER THREE
THREE-LIMB INDEPENDENCE

With the addition of the third limb into our drum kit playing, a whole new set of challenges comes into play. We must face this challenge by concentrating on a study of the human body I call "muscle memory." Muscle memory can be described as the body's ability to "memorize" and recall small movements. One common use of this facility is tying your shoes. When your mother or father first taught you to tie your shoes, they showed you how to make each loop and tie a bow and so on. Now, when you think of tying your shoe, you don't concentrate on each small movement involved but you think of the task as a whole. This is muscle memory. You have repeated these movements so many times that your body remembers all of the small movements involved in tying your shoe. We do this same technique when learning challenging independence movements on the drum kit. If you focus on the small pieces of the puzzle individually, the big picture will come together more quickly and, in time, more easily. When you hear someone playing a true three- or four-limb independence groove, it can sometimes be overwhelming. Don't get intimidated by this. Let's dissect it and conquer it!

We will be working on three-limb independence systems in this chapter. You will begin to see how all of the previous systems that we worked on are going to come into play. Drumming and music are compound learning systems. Nothing you learned in the beginning of study is forgotten. Everything you learned is added to and used as a foundation for new techniques. This is the main reason for always making sure not to skim over any part of your development. Anything you don't have total control over will only come back to cause you problems later. So, get it now and be done with it! When you add the third limb into drum kit performance, you will experience for the first time contra-rhythmic figures to each other. This means that at least one of your limbs will be in its own little world playing a rhythm that possibly does not interact with your other limbs. "Contra" is a form of the word "contradictory." This is just one way of saying you have to have the ability to not concentrate on this third limb. The brain cannot focus on three things at once. The brain can perform three things at once but cannot concentrate on all three. One of these has to be on "automatic pilot." This is independence.

The purpose of this three-limb section of *Transitions* is to get you used to letting one of your limbs go. Let the repetitiveness of these exercises formulate the muscle memory actions of your limbs. This is how we build the ability to let any limb play any figure we want at any time. This is a crucial time in practicing because your studies are only going to get more difficult. The next chapter on four-limb independence takes it to another level.

THREE-LIMB INDEPENDENCE
STRAIGHT-EIGHTH NOTES

The approach to these learning systems is the same as in the previous chapters. Now there is another element though. There is more than just choosing a riding pattern and playing through exercises. The amount of possibilities is multiplied due to the fact that there are riding hand patterns, kick drum patterns, and snare drum patterns to choose from. A riding hand pattern must always be chosen. If a kick pattern is chosen, then the exercise is to be read with the snare hand. If a snare pattern is chosen, the exercise is to be read with the kick foot. There will always be two ostinato patterns playing while another limb reads the exercise. This is true three-limb independence. Here is an example of a measure of a three-limb independence exercise assembled. This is Riding Hand Pattern #1, Kick Drum Pattern #1, and the snare reading the first bar of the one-note grouping exercise.

Here is an example of the kick drum reading the written figures. This is Riding Hand Pattern #3, Snare Drum Pattern #1, and the kick playing the first bar of the one-note grouping exercise.

The System Scratch Pad is included at the end of each system exercise group for the written assembly of patterns if needed. The most important factor of working through an advanced independence learning system such as this is the practical application. Each one of these riding hand, snare, and kick drum ostinatos are musical grooves and practical musical patterns. All of the systems in *Transitions* (other than basic linear patterns) are assembled together to form usable musical grooves. Throughout an average professional musical career, these combinations of patterns will surface again and again. This study time will create the facilities needed to execute difficult patterns in an efficient and musical manner. A good idea is to choose whether the snare drum or kick will play ostinatos first, and then choose a riding hand pattern and go for the exercise! Good luck!

THREE-LIMB INDEPENDENCE
STRAIGHT-EIGHTH NOTES
ONE-NOTE GROUPS

EXERCISE TRACK  **&**

RIDING HAND PATTERNS

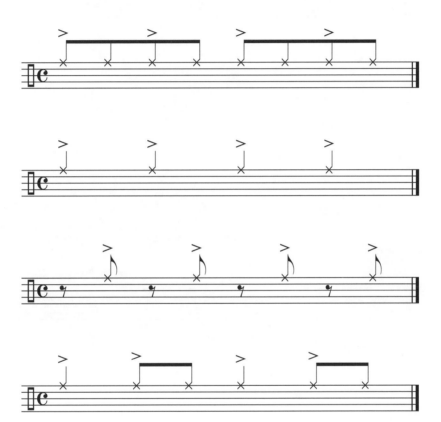

SNARE DRUM PATTERNS

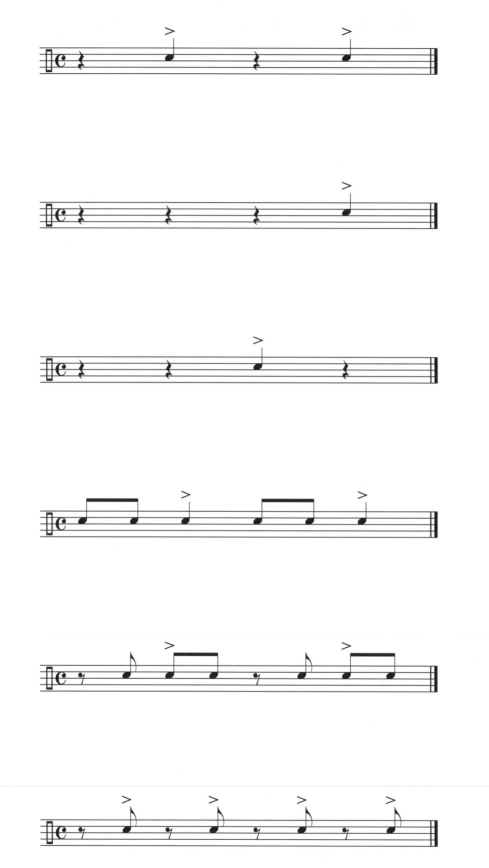

KICK DRUM PATTERNS

THREE-LIMB INDEPENDENCE EXERCISES
STRAIGHT-EIGHTH NOTES

DEVELOPMENTAL IDEA

This is an idea to help the development of these straight eighth-note exercises. Before attempting to play with the exercise play-along track, use a metronome (any click track) in ranges from 60 B.P.M. through to the tempo of the play-along (approximately 100 B.P.M.). Use a ten-bar practice format (similar to the one used in *The Drum Set Crash Course* book ghosting system). In the first bar, play just the riding hand; in the second bar add the kick pattern; and the third bar is the start of the eight-bar exercise that is written out for the snare. This will get the ostinatos in motion before the reading of the exercise begins. The same format can be used to work on the kick drum reading; just start the snare ostinato in the second bar.

EXERCISE TRACK

ONE-NOTE GROUPS

THREE-LIMB INDEPENDENCE EXERCISES
STRAIGHT-EIGHTH NOTES
TWO-NOTE GROUPS

Here is an example of one of the two-note group exercises assembled. This Riding Pattern #4, with Snare Pattern #5 and the kick, is playing bar 2 of the exercise.

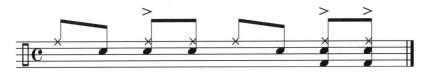

EXERCISE TRACK

THREE-NOTE GROUPS

Here is an example of a few of the three-note groups assembled with some ostinatos. This Riding Hand Pattern #2, with Kick Drum Pattern #3 and the snare, is the first bar of the three-note exercise. If needed, don't forget to use the System Scratch Pad at the end of these systems to assemble patterns.

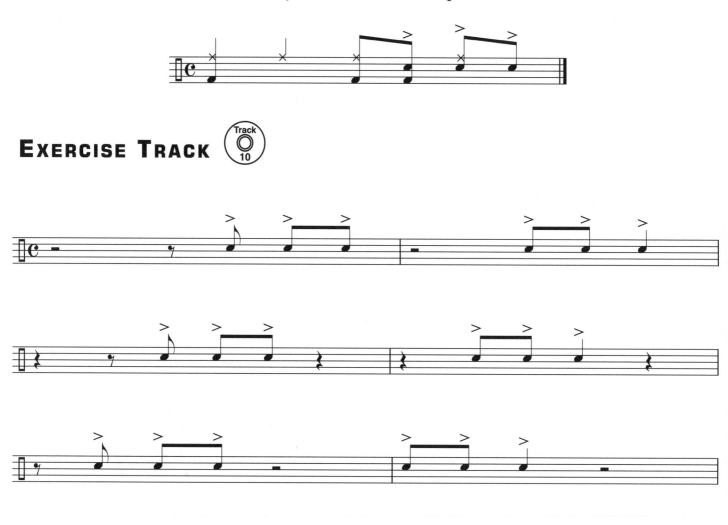

EXERCISE TRACK (Track 10)

FOUR-NOTE GROUPS

Remember to use the slight crescendo leading to the last note in the group of four-notes. This will add character to the figures and will sound more musical.

EXERCISE TRACK (Track 12)

Russ playing 73rd Oscars, 2001

THREE-LIMB INDEPENDENCE EXERCISES
32-BAR COMBINATION EXERCISE

EXERCISE TRACK

There are hundreds of combinations of patterns possible with all of the ostinatos and written figures. This combination exercise is a culmination of all of these. Choose the ostinatos for one limb and read this exercise with the others. Then switch limbs and do it again. There are several combinations for this exercise alone. It is possible to see now that there are very few possibilities of straight eighth-note figures that could be written in a composition that these studies didn't cover. Welcome to the wide world of independence!

SYSTEM SCRATCH PAD

THREE-LIMB MIX OF EIGHTH-NOTE PLAY-ALONG

EXERCISE TRACK Track 15 & Track 16

ROC-A-LONG

By RUSS MILLER, GANNIN ARNOLD
and JONATHAN AHRENS

THREE-LIMB INDEPENDENCE SYSTEM
EIGHTH-NOTE TRIPLETS

The three-limb eighth-note triplet systems return to the 12/8 time signature. The patterns in this system will cross several genres of music including blues, shuffles, jazz, Afro-Cuban, '50s rock, and modern pop. These exercises will build the facilities needed for playing several styles of music covered in *The Drum Set Crash Course* music style references. The figures have a definite swing to them because of the 12/8 time signature. This is apparent in the horn section figures on the exercise play-along track. Try to line up exactly with the horn section figures. The articulations are important as well, as was covered in previous chapters.

RIDING HAND PATTERNS

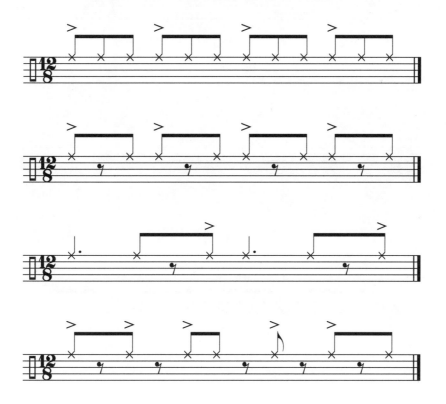

THREE-LIMB INDEPENDENCE
EIGHTH-NOTE TRIPLETS

SNARE DRUM PATTERNS

THREE-LIMB INDEPENDENCE EIGHTH-NOTE TRIPLETS

KICK DRUM PATTERNS

THREE-LIMB INDEPENDENCE
EIGHTH-NOTE TRIPLETS

EXERCISE TRACK  & Track 21

ONE-NOTE GROUPS

THREE-LIMB INDEPENDENCE
EIGHTH-NOTE TRIPLETS

EXERCISE TRACK (Track 23)

TWO-NOTE GROUPS

THREE-LIMB INDEPENDENCE
EIGHTH-NOTE TRIPLETS

EXERCISE TRACK

THREE-NOTE GROUPS

THREE-LIMB INDEPENDENCE
EIGHTH-NOTE TRIPLETS

EXERCISE TRACK (Track 27)

FOUR-NOTE GROUPS

THREE-LIMB INDEPENDENCE
EIGHTH-NOTE TRIPLET
36-BAR COMBINATION EXERCISE

EXERCISE TRACK

The 36-bar combination exercise is in a blues music style. The bass is playing a walking bass line. This form of bass line accentuates the quarter notes and makes it a little easier to keep time. Although this play-along has to be in a specific style, many of the grooves that are created from the pattern combinations form different music style grooves. All of the various combinations will work with this play-along exercise track. When the full eighth-note composition is played, a groove corresponding to that particular style should be played. Remember to listen for the horn section's articulations when working through the combination exercise. This exercise should be played reading the figures with the snare drum. Then go back and read the figures on the kick drum. Each of the riding hand patterns should be used to work through the 36-bar exercise. The combinations of all of the riding hand patterns and the snare/kick leading possibilities create many different combinations of this exercise.

THREE-LIMB INDEPENDENCE
EIGHT-NOTE TRIPLET
36-BAR COMBINATION EXERCISE

SYSTEM SCRATCH PAD

THREE-LIMB MIX OF EIGHTH-NOTE TRIPLET PLAY-ALONG

EXERCISE TRACK **&**

BIMINI

By RIQUE PANTOJA

THREE-LIMB INDEPENDENCE
SIXTEENTH-NOTES
ONE-NOTE GROUPS

EXERCISE TRACK  **&**

DEVELOPMENTAL IDEA

     This is the three-limb independence section for sixteenth notes. The systems are all getting progressively harder physically. If the physical challenges are too tough to play while executing the play-along tracks, work on the ten-bar practice concept discussed earlier. Working with the click track while playing just the ostinato limb patterns is the way to break down the physical problems. Just working on the riding hand and snare hand together with a click is a good way to start. Line-up is crucial, especially due to the number of notes in one bar of music. Work the tempos up to the tempo of the play-along track. Have fun!

RIDING HAND PATTERNS

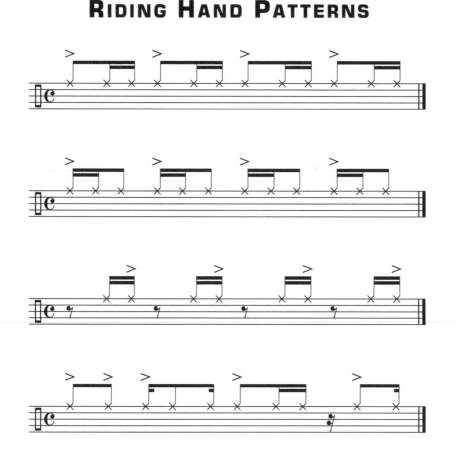

SNARE DRUM PATTERNS

KICK DRUM PATTERNS

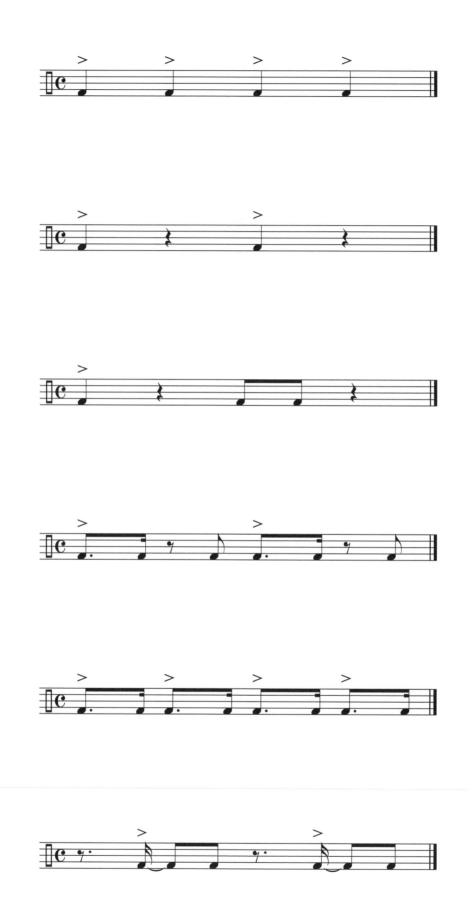

THREE-LIMB INDEPENDENCE
SIXTEENTH-NOTES
ONE-NOTE GROUPS

EXERCISE TRACK 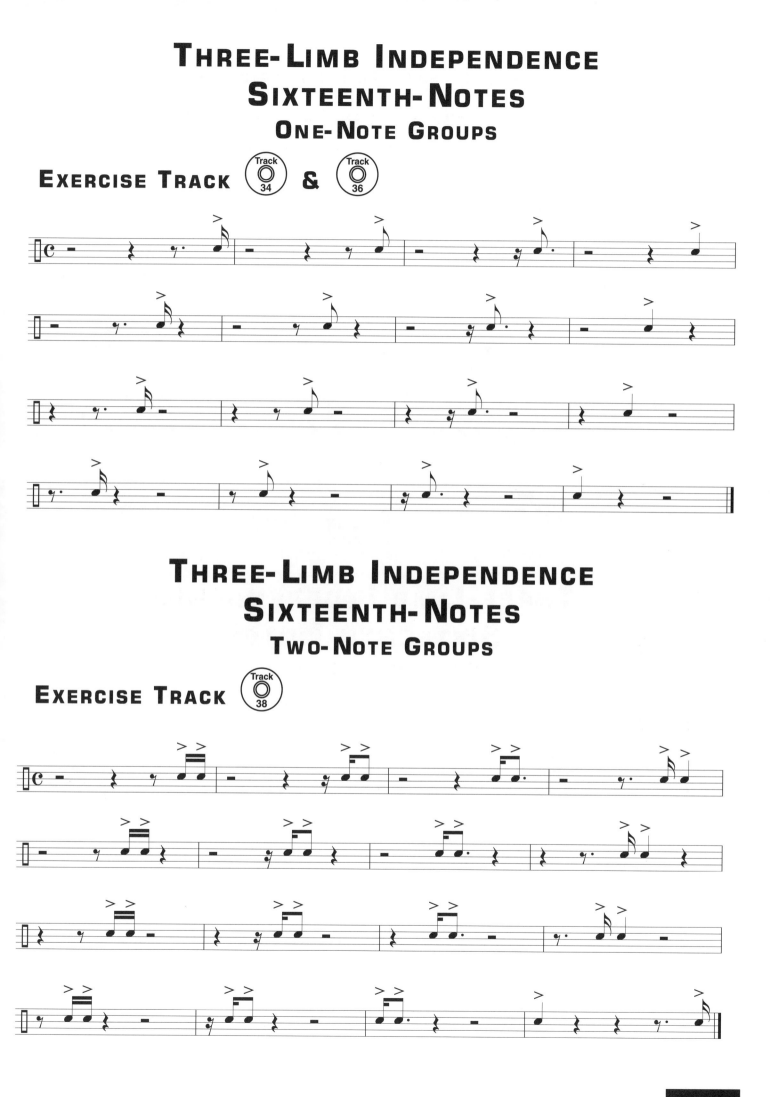 **34** & **Track 36**

THREE-LIMB INDEPENDENCE
SIXTEENTH-NOTES
TWO-NOTE GROUPS

EXERCISE TRACK **Track 38**

THREE-LIMB INDEPENDENCE
SIXTEENTH-NOTES
THREE-NOTE GROUPS

EXERCISE TRACK  **&**

THREE-LIMB INDEPENDENCE
SIXTEENTH-NOTES
FOUR-NOTE GROUPS

EXERCISE TRACK

THREE-LIMB INDEPENDENCE SIXTEENTH-NOTE 32-BAR COMBINATION EXERCISE

EXERCISE TRACK (Track 44)

    This exercise is the same concept as the 32-bar sixteenth-note combination exercise in the two-limb independence chapter. The percussion is hitting the figures written in the chart. Choose a riding hand pattern and a snare pattern and read the figures with the kick drum. Then choose a ride and a kick pattern and read with the snare drum. The combinations of all of the limb patterns and reading with different limbs create hundreds of variations of this one exercise. Use the System Scratch Pad for visually assembling troublesome sections of the play-along. Good luck!

THREE-LIMB INDEPENDENCE
SIXTEENTH-NOTE
32-BAR COMBINATION EXERCISE

SYSTEM SCRATCH PAD

THREE-LIMB MIX OF SIXTEENTH-NOTE PLAY-ALONG

BRINCADEIRA

By RIQUE PANTOJA

CHAPTER FOUR
FOUR-LIMB INDEPENDENCE

In this final chapter of *Transitions*, we will be focusing on the most difficult physical part of playing the drums. Four-limb independence uses all of the possible facilities of the body. When playing a true four-limb groove, we must focus on a few main points:

1. All of the limbs must be playing their parts independent of each other. You don't want one of your limbs to start following the others unintentionally.

2. All of the parts must line up with each other (as mentioned in previous chapters). The term "lining up" refers to every subdivision of the measure being played **precisely** with each limb. The notes happen exactly at the same point in time or, in other words, not sloppy. This can be one of the biggest challenges when playing complicated patterns. (For a further discussion of lining up, please refer to the funk chapter of *The Drum Set Crash Course* book.)

3. We must always approach these grooves from a music-first standpoint. Each limb has to groove on its own. Each part of the groove has to be self-sufficient, not relying on one of the other limbs. There has to be a musical reason for your attempting a four-limb groove, for instance, emulating four percussionists in an Afro-Cuban percussion section.

4. Each limb must have its own dynamic relationship to the whole. For example, just because the kick drum part is difficult doesn't mean it has to be loud!

5. The internal dynamics of your playing is very important. Whenever you play busier patterns, you must not sound "busy." If you sound too busy, it does not give the rest of the band the space they need to perform their parts. Ghost notes, accented notes, and moderate-level notes need to have a great amount of contrast. This is especially true for the ghost notes (unaccented notes that should be 1/2" stick heights). If these unaccented notes are very soft, they will cut down a great deal on how busy the groove sounds. There is an in-depth discussion on ghost notes and accented notes in the *Crash Course* book. To review some concepts on internal and external dynamics, refer to the feel discussion in *The Drum Set Crash Course* video.

The most important point to remember when learning this section of the book is not to get frustrated. These are serious physical challenges. Whenever you have to teach your body something, it takes a great deal of repetition. Four-limb independence will happen, but there is no shortcut. There are no easy paths to doing something great. Remember that you will have to deal with it later in your career anyway, so just get it out of the way now.

FOUR-LIMB INDEPENDENCE STRAIGHT-EIGHTH NOTES

The four-limb independence learning system is the most physically challenging aspect of playing the drum set. By adding the fourth-limb ostinato (the hi-hat played with the foot), there is a complete system of building the body's facility. Three limbs will be playing ostinato figures while one of the limbs reads the written figures in the exercises. The precision of each limb becomes crucial. The limbs must all line up perfectly or the grooves will be sloppy and useless in a musical context. Here is an example of a four-limb pattern. This is Riding Hand Pattern #1 , Kick Pattern #1, Hi-Hat Foot Pattern #1, and the snare reading the first bar of the one-note group exercise.

Each of the note group exercises and the combination exercise should be read through with each of the four limbs. Reading the figures with the hi-hat foot is very difficult and requires much practice. This is not a practical musical application, but it will free up that limb to be used in fills and solos. I work on this to develop consistent sounds with my hi-hat foot. This gives me the ability to use this limb in ways most players cannot. I recommend working on this. The key to successfully working through every combination of these exercises is patience. Don't get frustrated; this is difficult for everybody. The facilities gained through these exercises will make playing music much easier in the long run. Don't forget to use the scratch pad at the end of the system to notate troublesome combinations.

The following are the ostinatos to be chosen for the four-limb system.

FOUR-LIMB INDEPENDENCE
STRAIGHT-EIGHTH NOTE
RIDING PATTERNS

HI-HAT FOOT PATTERNS

FOUR-LIMB INDEPENDENCE
STRAIGHT-EIGHTH NOTE
SNARE DRUM PATTERNS

FOUR-LIMB INDEPENDENCE STRAIGHT-EIGHTH NOTE
KICK DRUM PATTERNS

FOUR-LIMB INDEPENDENCE
STRAIGHT-EIGHTH NOTE
ONE-NOTE GROUPS

EXERCISE TRACK  **&**

Here is a one-note group example. This is Riding Hand Pattern #3, Hi-Hat Foot Pattern #3, Snare Drum Pattern #1, and the kick reading the first bar of the exercise.

ONE-NOTE GROUPS

FOUR-LIMB INDEPENDENCE
STRAIGHT-EIGHTH NOTE
TWO-NOTE GROUPS

EXERCISE TRACK  **&**

Here is a two-note group example. This is Riding Hand Pattern #4, Hi-Hat Foot Pattern #4, Snare Drum Pattern #5, and the kick reading the first bar of the exercise.

TWO-NOTE GROUPS

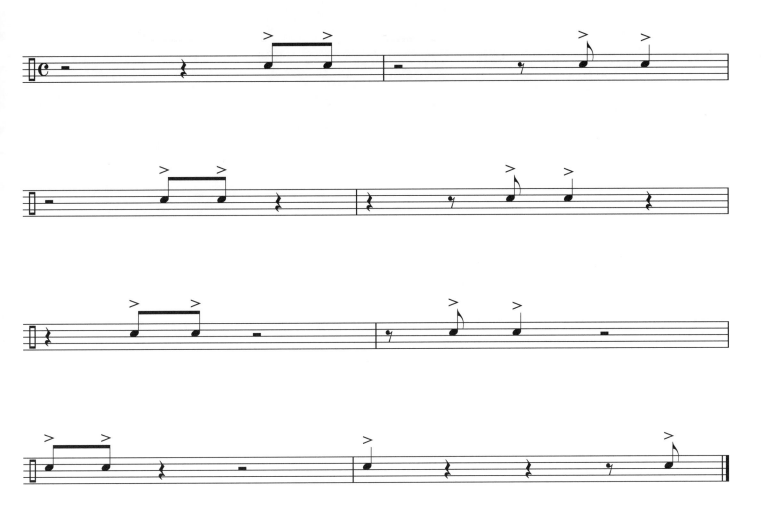

FOUR-LIMB INDEPENDENCE
STRAIGHT-EIGHTH NOTE
THREE-NOTE GROUPS

EXERCISE TRACK  **&**

Here is a three-note group example. This is Riding Hand Pattern #2, Hi-Hat Foot Pattern #2, Kick Drum Pattern #3, and the snare reading the first bar of the exercise.

THREE-NOTE GROUPS

FOUR-LIMB INDEPENDENCE
STRAIGHT-EIGHTH NOTE
FOUR-NOTE GROUPS

EXERCISE TRACK  **&**

FOUR-NOTE GROUPS

123

Four-Limb Independence
Straight Eighth-Note
32-Bar Combination Exercise

EXERCISE TRACK Track 13 & Track 14

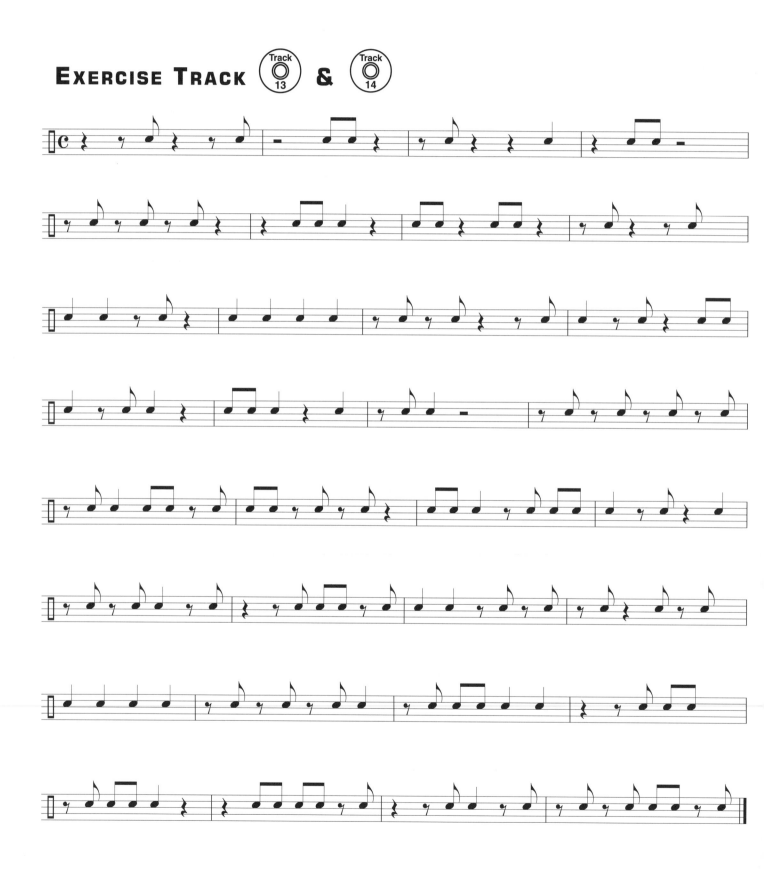

SYSTEM SCRATCH PAD

FOUR-LIMB MIX OF EIGHTH NOTE PLAY-ALONG

EXERCISE TRACK

ROC-A-LONG

By RUSS MILLER, GANNIN ARNOLD
and JONATHAN AHRENS

FOUR-LIMB INDEPENDENCE
EIGHTH-NOTE TRIPLETS

The same concepts of the straight-eighth note independence system apply to the eighth-note triplets version. Remember the swing factor of the 12/8 time signature that was discussed in previous sections.

RIDING HAND PATTERNS

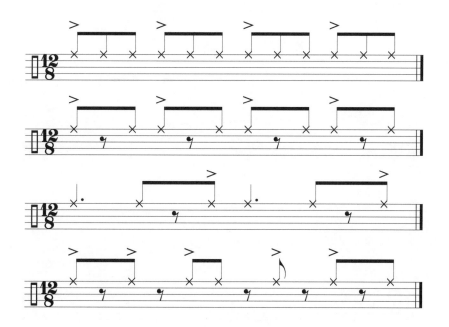

HI-HAT FOOT PATTERNS

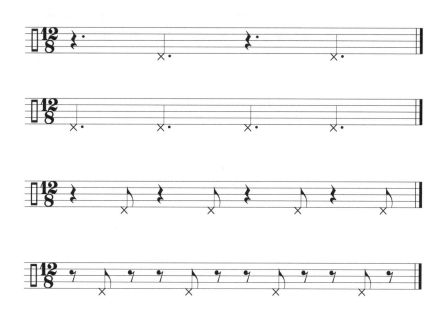

FOUR-LIMB INDEPENDENCE
EIGHTH-NOTE TRIPLETS

SNARE DRUM PATTERNS

FOUR-LIMB INDEPENDENCE
EIGHTH-NOTE TRIPLETS

KICK DRUM PATTERNS

FOUR-LIMB INDEPENDENCE
EIGHTH-NOTE TRIPLETS

EXERCISE TRACK Track 20 & Track 21

ONE-NOTE GROUPS

FOUR-LIMB INDEPENDENCE
EIGHTH-NOTE TRIPLETS

EXERCISE TRACK  **&**

TWO-NOTE GROUPS

FOUR-LIMB INDEPENDENCE
EIGHTH-NOTE TRIPLETS

EXERCISE TRACK

THREE-NOTE GROUPS

FOUR-LIMB INDEPENDENCE
EIGHTH-NOTE TRIPLETS

EXERCISE TRACK  &

FOUR-NOTE GROUPS

FOUR-LIMB INDEPENDENCE EIGHTH-NOTE TRIPLET 36-BAR COMBINATION EXERCISE

SYSTEM SCRATCH PAD

FOUR-LIMB MIX OF EIGHTH-NOTE TRIPLETS
PLAY-ALONG

EXERCISE TRACK

BIMINI

By RIQUE PANTOJA

136

FOUR-LIMB INDEPENDENCE SYSTEM
SIXTEENTH-NOTES
ONE-NOTE GROUPS

DEVELOPMENTAL IDEA

The four-limb independence section dealing with sixteenth notes is the most challenging in *Transitions*. This section incorporates true four-limb independence working through grooves that involve many styles of music. The limb patterns have been labeled by music style to demonstrate how these patterns will be used in musical settings. For more information about these various styles of music, refer to *The Drum Set Crash Course* text. This is very exciting; many grooves will be created that are used in professional music situations as well as some new grooves that will be formed out of your choosing. The key to perfecting this section is listening—listening to the play-along tracks for placement and time and listening to the limbs as they play four different patterns and attempt to line up perfectly. Finally, listen to the groove and music being created by each limb and the drum set as a whole. The mental focus you develop here will form your character as you practice this system.

RIDING HAND PATTERNS

Brazilian-influenced riding pattern

Fusion/disco riding pattern

Reggae riding pattern

Afro-Cuban cascara (in 4/4)

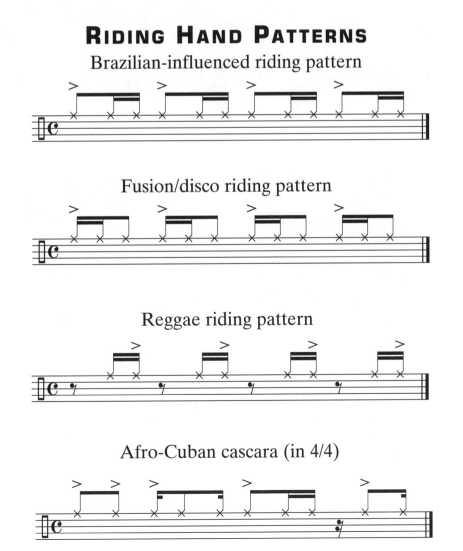

HI-HAT FOOT PATTERNS

Rock/Pop

Afro-Cuban/Double-Time Swing/Brazilian

Fusion/Funk

Cha-Cha-Cha/Solo Idea

SNARE DRUM PATTERNS

Rock/Pop Backbeat

Funky Pop/Afro-Cuban Backbeat

Half-Time Backbeat

Funky Ghosting/Disco Backbeat

Calypso/Afro-Caribbean/Brazilian Backbeat

Drum Set Crash Course Ghosting System/Fusion Backbeat

KICK DRUM PATTERNS

Disco/Dance/Pop

Funk/Rock/Pop

Rock

Brazilian Baião

Brazilian Samba

Afro-Cuban Tumbao

FOUR-LIMB INDEPENDENCE
SIXTEENTH-NOTES
ONE-NOTE GROUPS

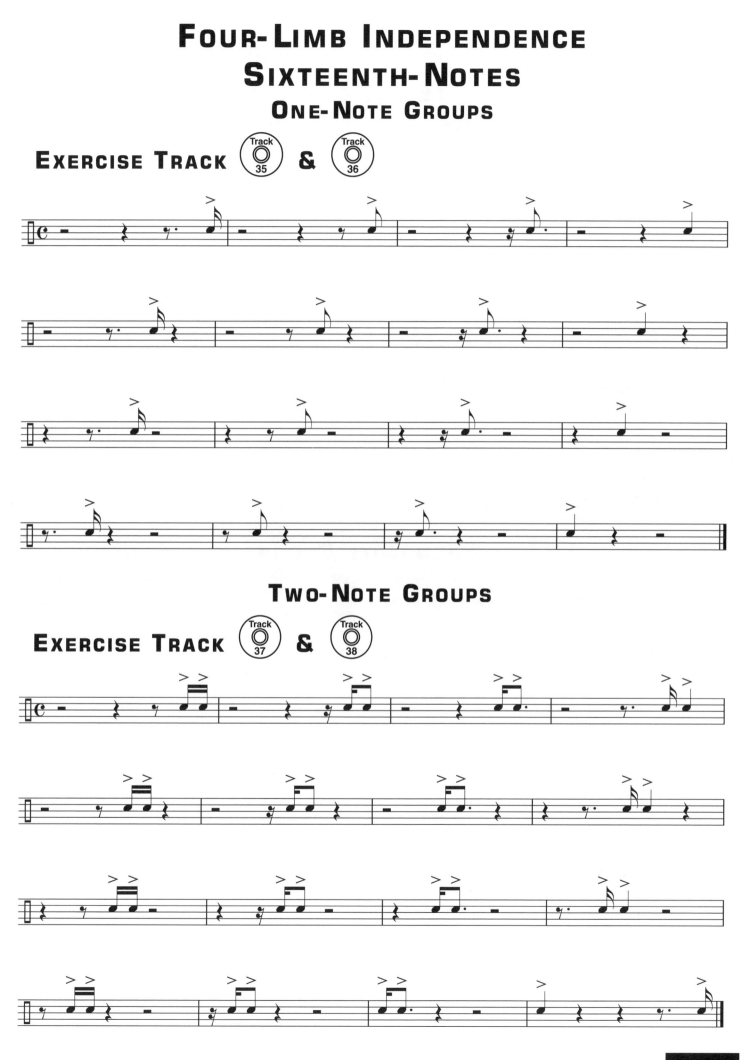

TWO-NOTE GROUPS

FOUR-LIMB INDEPENDENCE
SIXTEENTH NOTES
THREE-NOTE GROUPS

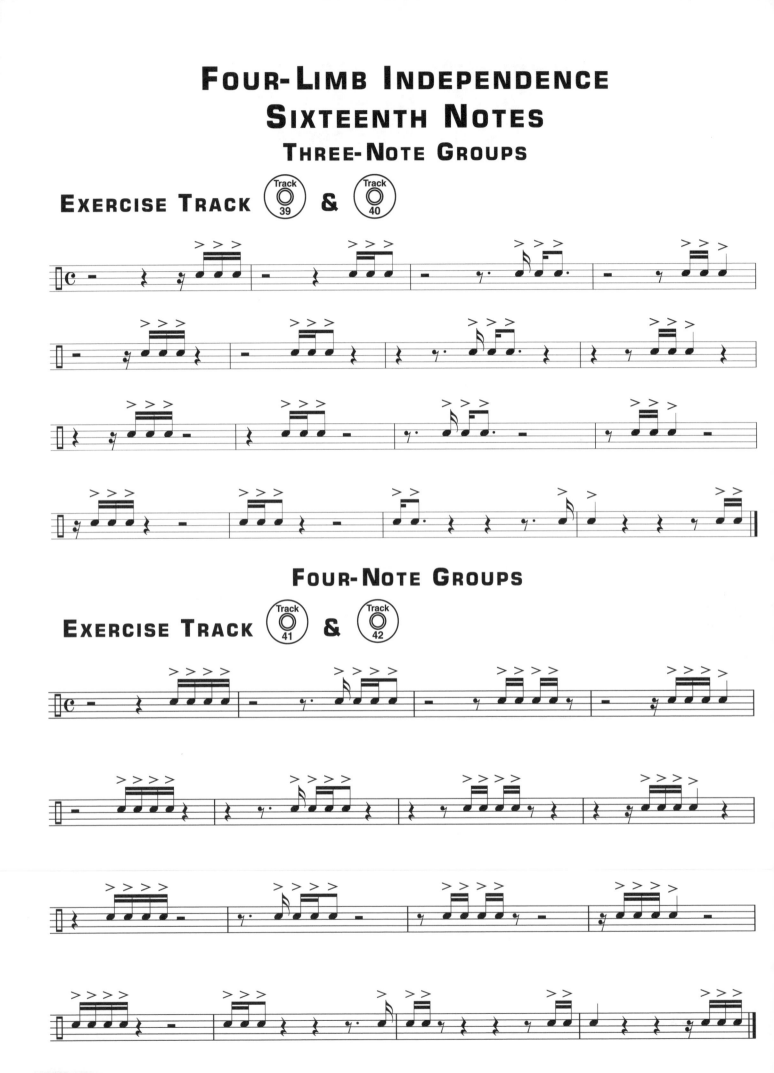

FOUR-NOTE GROUPS

FOUR-LIMB INDEPENDENCE SIXTEENTH-NOTE 32-BAR COMBINATION EXERCISE

EXERCISE TRACK (Track 43) & (Track 44)

FOUR-LIMB MIX OF SIXTEENTH NOTE PLAY-ALONG

EXERCISE TRACK &

BRINCADEIRA

By RIQUE PANTOJA

144